HISTORY *of* PHILOSOPHY

**Other works by Dr. Surrendra Gangadean
& The Logos Foundation:**

Philosophical Foundation: A Critical Analysis of Basic Beliefs
Theological Foundation: A Critical Analysis of Christian Belief
Philosophical Foundation: Trivium Study Guide
The Logos Papers: To Make the Logos Known

HISTORY *of* PHILOSOPHY

A Critical Analysis of Unresolved Disputes

SURRENDRA GANGADEAN

PUBLIC PHILOSOPHY PRESS ◆ THE LOGOS FOUNDATION λ LOGOS

Phoenix, Arizona

History of Philosophy: A Critical Analysis of Unresolved Disputes

Copyright © 2022 Surrendra Gangadean

Public Philosophy Press 2022
Phoenix, Arizona
publicphilosophypress.com

Printed in the United States of America

Cover design: Beth Ellen Nagle
Typesetting: Matthew P. Hicks & Brian J. Phelps

Library of Congress Cataloging-in-Publication Data pending

Gangadean, Surrendra, 1943–2022.
    History of philosophy: a critical analysis of unresolved disputes
    Includes bibliographical references, index, and glossary.
    ISBN: 979-8-9867472-2-4 (pbk.)

1. History of Philosophy 2. Philosophy—Basic Beliefs
3. Philosophy—Epistemology 4. Philosophy—Metaphysics
5. Philosophy—Ethics 6. Arguments for God I. Title

To the next generation

From those who are waiting, watching, and wishing

CONTENTS

EDITOR'S PREFACE

D R. SURRENDRA GANGADEAN (1943–2022), professor, pastor, husband, father, mentor, friend, and builder, was a giant in the faith and a Philosopher among philosophers. He spent a lifetime refining the foundation for philosophy (and theology and Historic Christianity). By recognizing the foundation, he was able to name the errors in the history of ideas due to the failure to have laid and built upon that sure foundation. He taught in the college classroom for 45 years, the seminary for over 25 years, and from the pulpit for almost 30 years. He taught Introduction to Philosophy, Logic, Ethics, Philosophy of Religion, Eastern Religions, World Religions, Introduction to Humanities, Philosophy of Art, The Great Books, Philosophical Theology, Biblical Worldview, Biblical History, Church History, Systematic Theology, Biblical Hermeneutics, and Existential Hermeneutics. In each of his encounters with notable thinkers and with his students, Dr. Gangadean heard, understood, and took intellectual challenges seriously. There was no known basic challenge that he did not work through—first for himself, then with others in much discussion, and then in his teaching and writing. He was tenacious in going after a basic dispute or challenge, finding the assumptions underlying the challenge, and then attempting a response and resolution of the problem.

History of Philosophy: A Critical Analysis of Unresolved Disputes (HP) is an example of Dr. Gangadean's incisive analysis of philosophical problems, which are rooted in unexamined assumptions, showing how he worked tenaciously to address those assumptions. He always begins with the assumption that some things are clear, the basic things are clear, the basic things about God and man and good and evil are clear to reason (the Principle of Clarity). Because the basic things are clear, knowledge is possible (vs. skepticism and fideism). His assurance that knowledge is possible is what drives him to seek to address challenges, which, when unresolved, result in skepticism. And skepticism, left to foment, leads to nihilism (meaninglessness). Dr. Gangadean keenly saw that the truth distorted leads to division (unresolved disputes), apostasy, decay, and cultural collapse.

Dr. Gangadean brings the history of philosophy into sharp focus in the conclusion to HP as he shows that he is not merely interested in resolving disputes, but that the history of philosophy is part of a larger ongoing spiritual war between belief and unbelief, which is currently coming to expression through the conflict between anti-theistic atheistic Cultural Marxism and theism. Either false assumptions will be exposed and overcome by reason, and a deeper foundation for philosophy laid, or reason will be rejected, and emotion and power will be used to further push an anti-theist atheist agenda in a now global context. Seriously addressing faulty philosophical assumptions, then, becomes a matter of individual, cultural, and civilizational life and death.

This is not just another history of philosophy text. HP is a blueprint for how to face the philosophical challenges of the past and present, wisely and courageously. Dr. Gangadean shows us the full range of basic assumptions, which are not many; he shows us how to use reason critically to analyze basic assumptions and test them for meaning—that if an assumption violates a law of thought, it cannot be thought, and is therefore meaningless, and cannot be true.

In HP, part of Dr. Gangadean's groundbreaking work includes: overcoming skepticism and fideism; showing that material monism, spiritual monism, and dualism are contradictory belief systems when examined critically by the use of reason; and showing that there is a moral law that is clear because it is based on human nature; comprehensive, because it includes all of our choices and actions; and critical, because it is a matter of life and death. In addition, Dr. Gangadean uses the Principle of Clarity to show where other philosophers fail to provide a foundation for philosophy (and with that, culture and civilization) because they either deny that knowledge of basic things is possible, fail to see and build upon the basic things, or fail to recognize the good for human nature. Future generations will consider this small book a giant step forward in laying the foundation for philosophy on solid bedrock. It is truly a gem, an intellectual work of enduring value.

For the past few years, Dr. Gangadean had been working on the second edition of his first and more complete publication, *Philosoph-*

ical Foundation: A Critical Analysis of Basic Beliefs (PF). He thought that he could merely add the history of philosophy section from his 1997–1998 Sabbatical writing as an additional chapter of PF. As he and I went over the Sabbatical material, we quickly realized that it was enough to justify a second book. I had the privilege of being Dr. Gangadean's research assistant during that Sabbatical, and am very familiar with the work he did during that time.

After his passing in February 2022, Dr. Gangadean left me as curator of all his books and papers. Some of his former students and congregants and I spent the summer combing through the 45 years' worth of (mostly handwritten and audio-recorded) material. We found a box with his handwritten notes from the 1997–1998 Sabbatical year. What I did not realize was that I was only familiar with the fourth part of HP on the history of philosophy and that there were three prior parts on epistemology, metaphysics, and ethics. In many ways, those three parts were an early formulation of *Philosophical Foundation*. Thus, I highly recommend that you read HP and PF as companion works.

Dr. Gangadean had a very clear outline for the book that he had intended to write on his 1997–1998 Sabbatical, and he had a year's worth of handwritten notes that filled in most of his outline, but there were missing pieces. In editing HP, I had to look into other areas of Dr. Gangadean's work to fill in those gaps. The first source I used was his college classroom handouts and recorded lectures from the same time period. The second source was *Philosophical Foundation*. And the third source was his handwritten notes from other contexts. The introduction and first part of the book were almost totally complete. There was one section on *reason in its use* and a section on *reason in us* that is quoted from PF. I had to pull from his classroom handouts and lectures for almost all of parts two and three.

All of part four was complete except for the chapter on Aristotle, which was taken from a lecture given at Logos Theological Seminary and edited by The Logos Foundation Editorial Board, and the final chapter on Critical Theory. In 1997–1998 we were hardly considering Critical Theory, but in the summer of 2020, it became the dominant philosophy of the day. Dr. Gangadean had approximately ten handwritten pages of notes that served as a summary and analysis of Critical Theory, only they were not formally ordered thoughts. These notes were almost a written meditation upon the most pressing challenge of our day. One of the most difficult tasks of my career thus far, was to take those thoughts and craft a chapter that followed his previous method of summary and critique. What I think you will see in the final chapter is Dr. Gangadean's mature thinking on the history of philosophy, how we ended up where we are today philosophically, and the dire need to take thoughts captive and lay a surer foundation for culture.

In addition to my editorial work, there are many others who have helped in the editing and publishing process; particularly helpful was The Logos Foundation Editorial Board, which Dr. Gangadean set in place prior to his passing. We are learning the value of coordinating and cooperating for the Good. Hopefully, we will soon be humming at high speed.

I challenge you to read *History of Philosophy: A Critical Analysis of Unresolved Disputes* with an attitude of seeking, integrity, and the hope that there are answers to the unresolved disputes that we have inherited from the failure to address basic questions through the critical use of reason.

—KELLY FITZSIMMONS BURTON
Curator and General Editor
Phoenix, Arizona
September 2022

OUTLINE

PART II: METAPHYSICS

Chapter 3: On What Is Eternal

1. Proof for the Existence of God
2. The Ontological Argument: There Must Be Something Eternal
3. The Cosmological Argument: Only Some Is Eternal
4. The Natural Teleological Argument: Order in the World Is by Special Creation, Not Theistic Evolution
5. The Moral Teleological Argument: Both Moral and Natural Evil Serve the Good
6. Foundation in General and Special Revelation
    i. God the Creator: His Existence and Nature
    ii. Creation Is Revelation
    iii. Special Creation
    iv. The Nature of Man
    v. The Original State of Creation
    vi. Hope/The Sabbath
    vii. Moral Evil and Sin and Death
    viii. Redemption
7. An Introduction to Christianity

PART III: ETHICS

Chapter 4: The Moral Law

1. The Concept of the Good
2. The Moral Law
    i. Moral Law 1: The Good and God
    ii. Moral Law 2: Thinking and Presupposition
    iii. Moral Law 3: Integrity and Knowledge
    iv. Moral Law 4: Work and Hope
    v. Moral Law 5: Authority and Insight
    vi. Moral Law 6: Human Dignity and Rationality

INTRODUCTION

THE HISTORY OF PHILOSOPHY IS BESET by unresolved disputes. These disputes are passed down from generation to generation as problems to be solved. If not solved, they engender skepticism. Philosophical disputes, posed as problems, can be resolved or dissolved if we first acknowledge that some things are clear to reason. Philosophical problems are about beliefs. There are more basic and less basic beliefs. All philosophical problems can be resolved by critical analysis of basic beliefs. What is basic is clear to reason. Basic beliefs are about God and man and good and evil. A historical, critical analysis of philosophical problems reveals what a thinker believes about reason, God, man, and the good for man. Not all basic beliefs are coherent when tested by the critical use of reason. A critical analysis of basic beliefs should lead us to see what is clear.

This book is written for those who have doubts about clarity, and for all who seek to know what is clear. It is written for all those affected by skepticism. It is written for those willing to critically examine basic beliefs and existentially examine their underlying assumptions. It is written to pave the way toward resolving longstanding disputes.

Naturally, basic questions like "what is it all about?" and "why am I doing this?" are forced into our consciousness for consideration. However, soon skepticism and cynicism may assert themselves, projecting our hopelessness upon all who ask. There is a necessity for clarity, whether or not seen within this text. What is clear is basic. What is basic concerns what is eternal and what is the good. What is clear is about God and the moral law.

Some things are clear. Some things are clear to reason. And it is because some things are clear that skepticism is without excuse. Skepticism doubts that some things are clear. Skepticism is not opposed to strongly held beliefs. Plato believed knowledge of the good is possible, but only to a very few. Thomas Aquinas believed knowledge of God is possible, but only to a very few. Neither believed that these basic beliefs were clear.

Skepticism is intellectual despair, which is the source of all other despair. Skepticism is rooted in uncritically held assumptions and is manifested in unresolved disputes, whether popular, historical, or philosophical. The way out of skepticism is to critically examine one's assumptions. Thinking is presuppositional. We think of the less basic in light of the more basic. If we agree on what is more basic, we will agree on what is less basic.

In what follows, an attempt will be made to critically examine assumptions to identify what sorts of things are more basic and what is clear about what is basic. I will try to identify the most basic elements in our thinking, those which make thinking possible: reason, being, causality, essence, substance, and unity. I will critically examine the basic views in metaphysics concerning what is real/eternal and in ethics concerning the good. I will argue it is clear that only some (being) is eternal and draw out the implications. And based on what is eternal, I will argue that it is clear what is the good and draw out implications for the moral law.

Presently, disputes about the possibility of knowledge persist between scientists and postmodern critics (between perennial naturalism and critical anti-realism). There are disputes between science and religion about biological origin and about the beginning of the universe. There are longstanding disputes between religions (Judaism, Christianity, and Islam, and Hinduism and Buddhism) and disputes within religions (Catholic and Protestant, Shi'a and Sunni, Theravada and Mahayana). There are disputes between rationalists and empiricists, between economic and political theorists, psychologists, and social scientists. There are disputes over gender issues, sexual morality, and human life (abortion, euthanasia, and genetic engineering). There are disputes between generations, between ethnic groups, and domestic disputes. There are even unresolved disputes within each person.

What all sides in these disputes have in common, which hinders resolution, are uncritically held assumptions. And what is needed to engage in critical examination of one's assumptions is a deeper level of integrity, or concern for consistency, intellectually and existentially.

I wish to overcome the debilitating effects of intellectual despair. Though we are all afflicted with skepticism to varying degrees and we are all called to self-examination, it is the special task of philosophy to critically examine assumptions. And though philosophers readily acknowledge that we are to begin with our own assumptions (Socrates is supposed to have said, "the unexamined life is not worth living"), as human beings, philosophers have the same resistance and struggles as others engaging in self-examination, perhaps more so. Those who teach have more vested in what they teach and are more humbled if what they teach is mistaken.

An assumption on which this work is based is that clarity is necessary for morality; that if some things (what is real and what is the good) were not clear, one could not be held responsible for one's beliefs and actions about good and evil. It could not be said we ought to have known better or done otherwise (there are other conditions necessary for morality; here, we are concerned only with clarity).

The kind of clarity I have in mind is objective clarity, what can be known by any user of reason, not what is actually known or clear to someone (subjective clarity). All who make choices have some beliefs about good and evil and, as such, ought to have used reason to critically examine the grounds of those beliefs.

The skepticism to which clarity is opposed is not just to those who claim to withhold assent to basic beliefs because they believe them not to be clear. Clarity is opposed to those who hold basic beliefs as a matter of dogma, to those who claim basic beliefs are a matter of faith (fideistic theism). It is likewise opposed to those who claim knowledge of basic beliefs about the real and the good is possible, but only to a few (Plato, Aquinas). It is also against those who hold false beliefs because of faulty assumptions (however sincerely one may feel), and it is against those whose beliefs may be true but whose rational support is lacking. Clarity is not common sense (Reid, Plantinga). Clarity shows the contradiction of what is clear—what is not logically possible—so that one has to deny reason (and therefore the possibility of thought) to avoid what is clear.

It would appear at first that this task of overcoming skepticism is too daunting, given the great number of disputes that there are and how longstanding these have been. It is quite the contrary, however, if skepticism is rooted in uncritically held assumptions. For it is not as if there are many such assumptions to be examined (there are relatively few that are basic), nor have those been subject to much discussion since they have been held uncritically and mostly unconsciously. What is daunting is achieving and sustaining the willingness to examine one's assumptions. What is daunting is the attainment of integrity, intellectual and existential. And it is only the consciously anticipated or actually experienced effects of the lack of integrity that moves us to greater depth of integrity.

Lack of integrity is experienced as disintegrity, or disintegration, personally and socially. From skepticism to cynicism, from anomie and ennui to complacency and apathy, we lurch crisis by crisis into the abyss until we lose all interest in asking "who am I?" or "where am I?" We are left with the self as void. And the bravado of embracing this void is itself void, utter despair. It is for this reason that skepticism or intellectual despair, the mother of all despair, requires urgent attention. There is hope only if some things are clear.

This book is divided into four sections. The first section identifies which things are basic in thought. The second and third attempt to show what is clear about what is basic. And the fourth critically examines the positions taken on basic issues by major philosophers in the schools of the Western and Eastern Traditions in an attempt to identify and settle longstanding unresolved disputes.

What is basic in thought is, first of all, what is necessary for thought itself. Thought is made possible by reason or the laws of thought. The term "reason" is used in several senses; the most basic sense of reason, as the laws of thought, is what is of interest here. Most discussions eventually break down over the limits of reason. What is more basic is the nature of reason itself and the extent of our use of reason. We may use reason while not being aware we are using it, and we may fail to use reason where we can use it. So, much scrutiny must be given to defining reason and its use.[1]

There are a few basic concepts with which the use of reason in thinking must begin. There is the concept of being, and what contrasts being with being, and what being assumes, including the concepts of substance, essence, and existence; the concepts of time, change, and causality; and the concepts of temporal and eternal, finite and infinite, changeable and unchangeable. These concepts make thought possible because thought is always about being or about what assumes being. These conditions for thought cannot be disputed without denying the

---

1. Surrendra Gangadean, *Philosophical Foundation: A Critical Analysis of Basic Beliefs, Second Edition* (Phoenix: Public Philosophy Press, 2022), 11-13.

possibility of thought itself. To deny the possibility of thought is to assert nothing. If nothing is being asserted, then no dispute can occur, since disputes require assertions.

In addition to concepts about being, there are concepts about the good which are grounded in acts of human beings. Concepts of ends and means and unity are inherent in choice. The good is what is sought for its own sake, as an end in itself, and it is the source of unity in a person, between persons, and between groups of persons. What are means to the good are considered virtues. And the effect of possessing what we believe is the good is happiness. Distinguishing and relating these concepts are essential to settling ethical disputes. And relating essential human activity to the good shows how the moral law is grounded in human nature and can be known by all.

In particular, I will attempt to show what is clear about what is basic. Beginning with eternal being as our most basic concept, I will argue that there must be something eternal, in contrast to various forms of none is eternal (all is becoming). This is the first truth about what is clear. Reaching an agreement that this is so will reveal where we are in relation to the use of reason and clarity and whether it is possible to go further.

If we cannot agree on what is more basic, then we will not agree on what is less basic in what follows. If we abandon reason to avoid what is clear, we give up thought and, with it, integrity and meaning. Here the journey begins or never begins. The choice is between reason and its denial, between thought and no thought. If "some is eternal" is not clear, there is no point in going further. To be casual at this point is to allow uncritically held assumptions to enter and to sow the seeds of intellectual despair. This first truth, known by reason, is the test of our understanding of the nature of reason and of our commitment to the use of reason. Under no condition should it be circumvented.

Continuing, I will argue for realism, that the material world exists (in contrast to various forms of idealism), but against naturalism, that the material world is not eternal. I will argue that minds exist, in contrast to material monism (which claims the mind is the brain) and in contrast to spiritual monism (which claims that ultimately one mind only exists), but that the mind (soul) is not eternal, in contrast to dualism (which claims that both matter and soul are eternal). Several disputes will be settled along the way, but the most basic dispute between theist ("only some is eternal") and non-theist ("all is eternal") will also be settled in favor of theism.

Thus, by combining an ontological argument that there must be something eternal with a cosmological argument that some things are not eternal, the conclusion is reached that God exists as Creator, not merely as Prime Mover or designer. In each argument, clarity is seen where one must deny reason to maintain the alternative position.

There are counterarguments against the existence of God. The two most common are from science and the problem of evil. Both are counterarguments based on the order in the world. The first claims that the natural order can be explained without God, and the second claims that the evil, or moral disorder, in the world calls the goodness of God into question and hence the existence of God. At least they together raise doubt that the eternal power and divine nature of God is clearly revealed. In both cases, I will argue that by critically examining assumptions and by agreeing on what is more basic, the disputes can be resolved or dissolved. I will argue that by examining assumptions about the principle of uniformity and its application, and by clarifying the nature of good and evil, and by distinguishing moral from natural evil, the counterarguments must be reformulated and resolved or dissolved at the more basic level.

Based on what is clear about what is eternal, I will argue that some things are clear about human nature and the good. And based on human nature and the good, I will argue that the moral law governing our affairs, both personal and social, can be known. Without agreement on what is more basic, knowledge of the moral law is hopeless. But with clarity about what is more basic, the moral law is easily knowable. The moral law speaks about the good and God, thinking and presupposition, integrity and knowledge, work and hope, authority and insight, human dignity and rationality, friendship and marriage, value and talent, truth and justice, and suffering and the good. The basis of each law in human nature is identified, and the implications are developed so as to form a coherent personal, social, and political philosophy.

In part four of this work, I will critically examine what several philosophers have said about what is basic and clear. I will consider how and why they differed with others and what influences they had. Among the philosophers I will examine are the views of the Presocratics, Plato and Aristotle, Nagarjuna and Buddhist philosophy, Augustine (and Augustinians such as John Calvin and Alvin Plantinga), Shankara and *Advaita* Vedanta philosophy, Ramanuja and *Dvaita* Vedanta philosophy, Thomas Aquinas, Rationalism (including Rene Descartes, Baruch Spinoza, and Gottfried Leibniz), Empiricism (including John Locke, George Berkeley, and David Hume), Immanuel Kant, Georg Hegel, Existentialism (including Soren Kierkegaard, Friedrich Nietzsche, Jean-Paul Sartre, and Albert Camus), Postmodernism, and Critical Theory, Marxism, and Virtue Ethics. I will confine myself to what each says about what is basic—about the possibility of knowledge, what is reason, what is real, and about what is the good. In doing so, I hope to make it clear that disputes arise from unexamined basic beliefs and that, upon examination, the truth about what is basic is clear.

PART I

EPISTEMOLOGY

Chapter 1

———

THE BASICS
IN THOUGHT

AN APOLOGY FOR PHILOSOPHY

THE MULTITUDE OF MANKIND FEEL they have little or no use for philosophy. If they do not find it slightly ridiculous, they casually ignore it and think it is reserved for only a few rather elite persons who are of an eccentric sort, that is, for philosophers. That feeling is not absent in much of the academic world and is found even among students who have had more than a course or two in philosophy. That feeling seems warranted since philosophy is seen to be an ivory tower activity far removed from ordinary life. There seems to be a disconnect between philosophy and life.

Yet, if philosophy is about anything, it is about the basic issues of life. An apology is therefore due to the public for the relevance of philosophy. It needs to be shown why *everyone must be philosophical*.

Knowing Good and Evil

Philosophy has to do with the nature of good and evil, which is as basic, important, and as universal an issue as we are likely to find. But it is the very nature of evil, if it exists, to distort the concepts of good and evil. It is no easy adversary to the good, but it is subtle, fierce, and unrelenting in its opposition to the good. Its highest achievement is to replace the good and to call good evil and evil good. It reaches everywhere and enlists in its service our highest strivings, even philosophy, religion, politics, science, and the arts. No one is beyond its reach.

Since philosophers are not exempt, we can expect the conflict of good and evil to penetrate philosophy, too, as well as the popular view of things. So, we are all called to discern good and evil, and we cannot rely on anyone to do so for us. Because of its subjective effects on each of us, the greatest care in critical reflection is required of each of us in discerning good and evil. Such critical reflection is the essence of philosophy, so each person has to be philosophical. We may make use of the reflections of others, especially of philosophers, but we cannot rely on them. *Everyone must be philosophical.*

Discerning good and evil is a necessary step to pursuing the good. But there are steps prior to and necessary for discerning good and evil. And there are additional and necessary steps afterward, too. We must understand human nature in order to know the good for man, and we must know the nature of reality to understand human nature. We must do metaphysics in order to do ethics. And we must understand the nature of knowledge before we can claim to know the nature of reality. Having done all this and having come to the knowledge of the good, we must also know how to achieve the good; that is, we must have knowledge of the moral law. Discerning good and evil lead to the whole range of issues which are the core concerns of philosophy. Suddenly it all seems a bit much, even if it is all necessary. We face a basic and recurring temptation to despair of having knowledge and to yield to skepticism. Most men seek to avoid the pit of skepticism by lapsing into tradition or accepting claims of divine revelation by faith.

Neither skepticism nor tradition nor faith avoids taking a position on the nature of knowledge and simply holds its position uncritically, the opposite of what is needed if we are to avoid a false view of good and evil. Skepticism denies that some things are clear. This denial is rooted in uncritically held assumptions. If some things are not clear, objectively clear to reason, then there is no justifiable distinction between good and evil. And the distinctions made, whether by tradition or by faith, are therefore not justified and are therefore of no value. If good and evil exist, they must be objectively clear, along with all that is necessary to know it. To think that what is objectively clear must also be subjectively clear is naively to deny the possible effects of evil on our willingness to see the truth about the world and ourselves. There is, therefore, no escape from having to be philosophical, whether in skepticism, or tradition, or faith. *Everyone must be philosophical.*

Life and Death

If philosophy is concerned with good and evil, it is also concerned with life and death, which are the non-physical or spiritual effects of pursuing good and evil. Since the spiritual condition of life or death is inescapably present in everyone, everyone has to seek life and avoid death, however this may be conceived, subjectively. Without doubt, having meaning is necessary for life, and meaninglessness is a condition of spiritual death. Minimally, meaning occurs when things make sense, when there is coherence in our understanding, and when there are no transparent contradictions in what we think and do. Our beliefs cannot be true and not true at the same time and in the same respect. We cannot act and undo our act repeatedly and indefinitely without being or becoming insane. Meaning requires rationality in both a logical and a practical sense.

Life requires meaning and is constituted by meaning. The more meaningful our world becomes, the more we are full of life. Meaning comes as we exercise our understanding, and understanding requires the use of reason. By reason, we test our beliefs for coherence of meaning, and by reasoning, we grow in understanding. Life for man is bound up in the use of reason. The fullness of life requires the full use of reason. Everyone who seeks the fullness of life must use reason fully. *Everyone must be philosophical.*

If the use of reason brings meaning and life, then the failure to use reason or the denial of reason brings meaninglessness and death. We often do not recognize contradictions in our basic beliefs unless our understanding is put to the test. Then what appeared to be meaningful loses its meaning. The more we become conscious and consistent with a contradictory basic belief, the more life is emptied of meaning. Without meaning, life becomes boring, and we seek escape through self-indulgence and mindless activities. To think that our deepest suffering, caused by meaninglessness and boredom, is brought on by our own failure to use our reason brings guilt of the deepest sort and sends us in search of other explanations by which to justify ourselves and alleviate the guilt. Since meaninglessness, boredom, and guilt are common to all men and are conditions against which we must strive, *everyone must be philosophical.*

A Worldview Is at Stake

What puzzles most people is seeing the connection between the fine points and the main points, between the details and the fundamentals. The fundamentals determine the details, and the details express the fundamentals. Intellectuals argue about details as if their life depended on it, and it does. They, more than others, see that we think in systems in which all points are connected. What is at stake in the details is the entire system, a whole worldview, and that is what makes the arguments so passionate. It would be naive to think that ego and money could not be involved, but it would be cynical to think they are all that is involved. A worldview is what is at stake.

A worldview includes everything; it includes all aspects of culture and every dimension of life. A worldview is a system of meaning and values built upon a set of basic beliefs, the implications of which are applied to every detail of life. It is incomplete if it remains on a general level; it comes to reality only in the details. The devil, it is said, is in the details. In religion, it reaches to the words of our mouth and the meditations of our heart. A view of human nature has implications for freedom and responsibility, which come to expression in attitudes towards abortion, capital punishment, and psychotherapy.

While many take to the streets in passionate protests, a few deliberate in think tanks and one or two write essays on the fundamental principles of morals. The latter shape the former. The architect anticipates every use of the finished structure. The shape and strength of the house of culture in which we each live is determined by the foundation laid. If the house is built on the sand and it collapses in the storm, surer foundations are needed. Since everyone lives in some house, and every house needs sure foundations, everyone must be sure of their foundations. *Everyone must be philosophical.*

The Good Requires Unity

No man is an island. We are all part of the mainland. For better and for worse, we inherit the cultural strivings of all men, build upon them, and transmit them to the generations to come. The cultural goal we seek is in progress. It is too vast to be accomplished by one or even by some. It takes the entire race of men, in the most intricate web of yearning and striving, to develop the powers latent in mankind and in the world. The waste of talent is a loss for all; its flowering is a thing of beauty and a joy forever. Each contributes uniquely. The destroyers of culture require more from its builders and get it. So, progress is made.

The goal of mankind is the good. It satisfies the deepest desires of the heart. It is comprehensive and inexhaustible. It is corporate, cumulative, and communal. It increases with sharing. It requires the unity of men in their diversity rather than the division of men in their differences. The striving to overcome divisions is the most demanding part of cultural life and its results are the most rewarding. Here, hope agonizes in its struggle with despair. That good will overcome evil is the interest of each person however blind and confused the battle may be. Each must receive from all and each must contribute to all in order for each to enjoy the good fully. Since everyone has an interest in the good, and everyone must strive for the unity of all, *everyone must be philosophical.*

The Power of Ideas

It is better to suffer in doing good than to do evil. Wars have been fought throughout history. Some wars have been fought for centuries. Some conflicts seem destined to last for centuries. In the long run, nothing is settled by war because the battle is one of ideas, and bombs cannot destroy ideas. Many suffer in war, but war is not necessary. Many suffer in vain in war thinking it may do good. Many are willing to suffer in war rather than suffer to understand and address the ideas which cause war.

It is better to suffer to destroy a false idea than to destroy a person. False ideas cause war when they are not destroyed. True ideas do not cause war and they cannot be destroyed. When we destroy false ideas, we liberate persons held captive by the false ideas. As long as there are false ideas, intellectual wars are necessary. Physical wars are fought when we fail to fight the intellectual wars.

To fight an intellectual war, we must avoid being taken captive by false ideas. And we must be prepared to demolish arguments and pretensions raised up against the truth. Intellectual wars require stren-uous training in the use of reason. Demagogues and propagandists lose their following when their falsehoods can be seen through and exposed. It is better to suffer in doing good than to do evil. Since wars affect the multitudes, everyone must strive to engage in intellectual war in order to avoid the futility and evil of physical war. *Everyone must be philosophical.*

Arguing Without Integrity

Because so much is at stake in arguments and because in arguments there is an existential conflict of good and evil, arguments are often not as clean and tidy as they might be. Quibbles, subterfuges, and obfuscations abound. There are embarrassing silences. Exposure is painful without the willingness to admit error. One's order of good and evil is being reversed. At times one's life hangs by the thread of an argument and a person must be willing to lose their life in order to gain it. What was seen as natural must now be surrendered as vice. What was once treasured must be flung away as a hindrance. When one is not willing to change one's basic belief, resistance deepens. There is more self-deception and self-justification. We strain at gnats and swallow camels. We kill the messenger to avoid the message. If one's own view is not true by reason, then no view is true because knowledge is impossible. Reason is declared fallible or limited or fallen, and a hindrance in encountering the highest reality, or, for that matter, in knowing any reality. The history of philosophy is full of dead messengers, who come in the name of reason. But not only philosophy.

Everyone, when encountered by what is clear, seeks an excuse for not having seen it. And excuses persist until we reach the most basic level of thought, at which point reason itself must be given up to save one's belief and to avoid acknowledging what is objectively clear. But reason is the laws of thought itself, and makes any thinking possible. Since we cannot hold a belief of any sort and give up reason, and since we cannot live without beliefs, we can only deceive ourselves into thinking we are doing so. At this point, we can only give up our integrity, if we do not give up our false beliefs.

If we are willing to critically examine our assumptions for meaning, we need not get into this predicament. Alternative assumptions will appear by which we can avoid the dilemma of antinomies (a pair of opposing beliefs, which may both be false because both share the same faulty assumption). We can also avoid the futility of affirming a belief to be true, which has been emptied of meaning. Since everyone is subject to the temptations of subterfuges or abandoning integrity, and since the way out of this temptation is to critically examine one's assumptions for meaning, *everyone must be philosophical.*

Not everyone will resist this temptation, and not everyone will be philosophical. Few, if any, readily avoid holding beliefs uncritically. We are often compelled to think deeply by what we suffer. And all men suffer. We suffer the natural evil of toil and strife, and old age, sickness, and death. These are contrary to our natural desires and do not appear to be necessary, however much we are accustomed to them, and however universal they may in fact be. We can conceive of a world in which these do not exist, and, in fact, we long for such a world. Natural evil may intensify into famines, wars, and plagues, as well as the occasional ravages of nature. While some escape some forms of natural evil, no one who survives escapes old age, sickness, and death. Death is the universal lot of all men, and death presses upon each one most fully the questions of our origin and destiny, and of good and evil.

There is an ordinary connection between our suffering and our failure to think. Insofar as we seek comfort above truth, we show we require suffering to get us to think. The sources of our comfort must be removed from us before we seek further. Sometimes the possibility of these comforts must be fully removed before we stop seeking them. We may harden ourselves under suffering even as we may attempt to deny reason, but to do so invites the increase of natural evil. Our failure to think and to see what is clear is without excuse and is the origin of moral evil. Natural evil, as a call to stop and think, is naturally connected to moral evil. It serves to restrain, recall from, and remove moral evil. Since natural evil is a call to stop and think deeply about basic issues, and since all suffer natural evil, *everyone must be philosophical.*

ON SKEPTICISM

In this section, we will examine the concern about skepticism, forms of popular skepticism, some common sources of skepticism, and forms of pseudo-arguments that perpetuate skepticism. Lastly, we will examine the two most common ways in the history of philosophy of overcoming skepticism—Rationalism and Empiricism.

The Concern About Skepticism

What is at stake in skepticism is intellectual despair that merits our attention. Briefly, it is the inextricable connection between intellectual despair and all other forms of despair, and the connection between despair and human suffering that merits our attention. Skepticism and suffering are connected in several ways. First, skepticism fails to overcome human credulity (fideism) and its attendant misery. Second, it allows us to build on faulty foundations (unexamined assumptions) that collapse and by which we suffer loss. Third, the lack of integrity, in an unwillingness to critically examine one's assumptions, invites suffering as necessary to get us to think deeply about our lives. Fourth, the meaninglessness which comes from a denial of the possibility of knowledge is a form of spiritual death. Fifth, social disorder results from skepticism, which denies that there are any justifiable moral standards for our lives together.

Skepticism and Fideism

Far from helping to eliminate suffering, skepticism increases it. The opposite of fideism is not skepticism, but clarity. Skepticism presents itself as the antidote to credulity, blind faith, superstitions, quackery, bigotry, and intolerance. But the exposure of these by what is clear is the true antidote and not skepticism. Ironically, fideism (belief without knowledge) is the antinomy of skepticism. They are two sides of the same coin because they both share a common assumption that knowledge is impossible or that nothing is clear. If knowledge is not possible, then it cannot be known that certain beliefs are false, not even that these beliefs are probably false. In that case, what one believes is a matter of personal preference. Skepticism thus opens the door to all beliefs as equal. If it is argued that skepticism urges us to withhold all belief, this is not humanly possible. And, in any case, we would need an argument to support the position that withholding belief is better than giving assent, something a conscientious skeptic could not do. Better for what, it may be asked, an unknowable good?

Skepticism and Foundation

Skepticism is rooted in uncritically held assumptions. Is it necessary to examine one's assumptions? Our lives as thinking human beings are built on foundational beliefs. We often simply and uncritically assume certain things to be true and precede from there. We often take common sense, intuition, and tradition (including what is currently fashionable in prestigious academic centers) for granted and go from there. We cannot avoid thinking and we cannot avoid building on some ground or another. No living person is without assumptions. The skeptic is not without assumptions, but is one led by his assumptions to conclude that nothing is clear. The question is whether we are building on a solid foundation, whether we are building on rock or on sand. We can and ought to examine our assumptions as we would examine the foundation of a house to see if we are building on what is solid. It is not merely optional or nice to think critically, to test our foundations. It is necessary if we are to avoid losing our efforts. Marriages collapse. Children go astray. Careers stall. Disappointments embitter. Life becomes weary, dull, stale, and flat. A true opinion or lucky guess does not have the firmness of knowledge. When challenged, we can be forced to abandon mere opinion, or limit its relevance to what is private, or harden into prejudice. If we do not test our assumptions at the beginning of taking responsibility for our lives, then they will be tested later by the demands of reality. Then it will be too late to avoid suffering loss from the collapse of what we have been building.

It may be objected that there is comfort in faith and tradition. Many thoughtless people seem quite happy while thoughtful persons often bewilder themselves to no avail. This description of these two as the only alternatives assumes what is basic is not clear, so why bother trying to know? The response is that we all face the human condition. Toil and strife, and old age, sickness, and death are common to all. We can try to avoid the angst of human existence by not thinking much. But a semi-comatose or infantile condition is contrary to our nature and is not lasting. It can be penetrated by intensified suffering or avoided only by hardening oneself.

Skepticism and Integrity

Skepticism, we have been saying, is rooted in uncritically held assumptions. Socrates is supposed to have said, "the unexamined life is not worth living." It appears we need a Socratic gadfly to keep us honest, to remind us of the obvious by asking: have you examined your assumptions lately? We make knowledge claims, unavoidably. We thereby profess to others an interest in knowing. We like to think that we are interested in knowing. Yet we neglect, avoid, and sometimes resist examining our assumptions. Why is this so? First, if our lives are comfortable, we do not want to change anything. Second, we have vested a great deal in getting to where we are, and we do not wish to lose our investment. Third, it would be painful to admit we are mistaken, particularly if we have been regarded as teachers. This is especially true if we have failed to see what is clear. There would be a lack of integrity in our professed interest in knowing.

Lack of integrity is immediately experienced as shame subjectively and guilt objectively. We know ourselves to be rational, and we know we ought to be concerned to know, and we ought to be consistent in what we say and do. Shame and guilt are too painful to bear. They affect our self-worth and our standing with others. We must acknowledge the truth about ourselves and turn from our way or try to cover it up from ourselves and from others. To cover it from ourselves requires self-deception, and to cover it from others requires self-justification with its perpetual excuse-making. So, to preserve ease of life and ease of conscience, we avoid self-examination. To get us to stop and think, we must be made uneasy; we must experience disease in body and mind. Skepticism, with its unexamined assumptions, invites and requires suffering in body and mind.

FORMS OF POPULAR SKEPTICISM

Knowledge has been defined as justified true belief. Justification may be *prima facie* (weak), or *ultima facie* (strong).[1] Skepticism is the denial that we can have knowledge. It is to deny that some things are clear to reason. Popular skepticism is the way most people end up in

---

1. Surrendra Gangadean, *Philosophical Foundation: A Critical Analysis of Basic Beliefs, Second Edition* (Phoenix: Public Philosophy Press, 2022), 51-52.

skepticism, it is popular, easy, and common. We will examine seven sources of popular skepticism.

There Are So Many Views

The claim that "there are so many views" is the first source of popular skepticism. Just look around, there are so many views. Philosophers do not agree—Plato and Aristotle did not agree. There are many religions in the world. If we could have known, we would have known by now. On the face of it, there are so many views and we cannot know. The response is that there are not many basic views. There is a view, and there is a basic view. A basic view is about what is eternal. There are only two basic views—either "all is eternal" or "only some is eternal." Both of these cannot be true, and both cannot be false. We can overcome the "many views" by recognizing there are only two basic views.

Furthermore, there are many degrees of rational consistency with which a basic view is held. A basic view is that God exists. Secondary views are Judaism, Christianity, Islam, and Deism, all which say that God exists. Judaism has five main forms, Christianity three, and there are many divisions within each. These divisions are not basic, but are degrees of consistency with which basic views are held. We are concerned with critically examining basic views.

All Views Are the Same

Some people say it doesn't matter anyway which view you hold. They are all the same. For example, don't all people hold to something like the golden rule? The form may be the same, but the content is different. "Do unto others as you would do unto yourself," but how do we understand the self? How we understand "the self" depends on our basic beliefs.

To say that it doesn't matter, all views are the same, may be true on a practical or psychological level, but even here only in the short run. Does it matter who you marry? Does it matter what they believe? Does it matter where you live? Of course, these things matter. Living in another culture where there are big differences matter. If large-scale, long-term differences in human lives are not important then nothing is important, including anything we say.

Who Is to Say?

Some may ask, "who is to say which view is right?" Often adding, and "who are you to say it?" This source of popular skepticism brings up the question of authority. Are you the authority? Is anyone? The assumption is that authority is personal, not rational.

The response to this is, "it is not who is to say, but what is to say." Reason—the laws of thought in all of us—must be observed if we are to avoid talking nonsense. Reason is natural, all of us can and should use reason at a basic level. Reason is transcendental, it is the source of authority. Reason is to say which view is right.

It Is All a Matter of Interpretation

Another popular skeptical claim is that "it is all a matter of interpretation." You have your interpretation. I have my interpretation. Everybody has their own interpretation of the Bible. Everybody has their own interpretation in literature. Postmodernism says there is nothing in the text itself, it is what the interpreter brings that gives meaning.

We can affirm it is true, it is all a matter of interpretation, but philosophy does not end here—it begins here. Every interpretation must be tested for rational consistency. If one says, "it's all a matter of interpretation," where does that get us? We should examine each interpretation to see if it is consistent.

It Is All Relative

Some say, "it is all relative." Of course, it is all relative. Relative to what? Culture? Culture is shaped by basic beliefs. It is all relative, to one's own basic belief. Basic beliefs can and should be tested for meaning.

I Do Not Know What I Believe

Some say, "I don't know what I believe." That does not mean we do not have a basic belief. We do have basic beliefs held more or less consciously. We can know our basic beliefs by looking at our actions.

I'll Go With the Flow

Some say, "I'll go with the flow." This is the simple, easy, what comes natural, approach. We can respond by saying go ahead, go with the flow. Perhaps we will meet again. The flow takes you over the deep end. Solomon said, in the Book of Proverbs, that disaster comes suddenly for the simple. Then they cry out for wisdom, but wisdom does not answer them.

The popular sources of skepticism are not adequate; we must address the more serious forms of skepticism.

COMMON SOURCES OF SKEPTICISM

Skepticism (intellectual despair) is rooted in our uncritically held assumptions. These assumptions may be part of our personality and temperament, or they may be part of our background and upbringing. And, unless we become more conscious of our assumptions, and strive with integrity to overcome and change, we will fall back into our old ways. Self-examination will help us to see how these sources of skepticism may be deeply embedded in our thinking. Each of the following sources of skepticism has one or more uncritically held assumption.

Informal Fallacies

Informal fallacies involve the use of irrelevant appeals as a substitute for the use of reason and logical argument. Some examples of informal fallacies include: *ad hominem*; straw man; question begging; appeal to pity, fear, popularity, etc. (see following section on informal fallacies). Use of informal fallacies assumes that if pseudo-argument does not succeed, no argument will succeed. We ought to identify informal fallacies in our own thinking first, and then identify them when we encounter them elsewhere.

Tradition and Custom

Tradition and custom, as a source of skepticism, assumes that what we are most comfortable with is true. Truth is comfort. For example:

Since it has been around a long time it is true; it is right because that is the way I have been taught. Most people I know think and act this way, etc. Certainty about our own tradition melts in our exposure to other cultures or hardens into prejudice. Both options are undesirable and unnecessary if we recognize that tradition and custom are not sources of knowledge.

Common Sense

Common sense becomes a source of skepticism when it assumes that appearance is reality (naïve realism). For example: The earth is flat; the sun rises in the east; the color of the ocean is blue, green, gray, clear. Common sense takes the condition of the perceiver for granted. What one experiences as appearances must be interpreted. Experience is not a source of knowledge.

Intuition

Intuition, as a source of skepticism, assumes that the natural sign is always accompanied by the reality, or the sign is the reality. For example: Truth is beauty, beauty truth; pleasure and goodness; sex and love; smile (good vibrations) and friendliness. It assumes this is a morally ideal world. In a morally ideal world, the sign would always accompany the reality, but this is not so in a world where evil exists. At best, intuition is a tool for reading signs, but it is not a source of knowledge. The psychological certainty that often accompanies intuitive insight is not the same as objective clarity. One may be sincere in belief and be sincerely wrong.

Science

Science is being misused and becomes a source of skepticism when its methods are overextended to a philosophical principle. Science becomes a source of skepticism when empiricism is assumed. Empiricism is the view that all knowledge is ultimately from sense experience, and that there are no innate ideas of reason apart from experience.

Science becomes a source of skepticism when it goes beyond its empirical boundary (in assuming only natural or material forces must be used to explain phenomena); when it fails to distinguish data (pure experience) from fact—data interpreted in light of philosophical assumptions; when it fails to notice that science does and must have philosophical foundations which have to be critically analyzed for coherence of meaning; and when skeptical disclaimers (tentativeness and pragmatism) are used to forgo philosophical criticism of its assumption.

Reason

Reason is a source of skepticism when it is misused or not fully used. Reason is misused when used as a source of truth rather than as a test for meaning. It is not fully used when it is used constructively only, and not first and fundamentally used critically to examine basic assumptions for coherence of meaning.

By becoming more conscious of our uncritically held assumptions and by becoming more consistent in the use of reason, we can avoid these sources of skepticism and associated longstanding disputes.

FORMS OF PSEUDO-ARGUMENT

Skepticism may arise from pseudo-arguments or informal fallacies. Often, we think we have attempted to argue for a belief, but the argument ended up not being productive, and our doubt deepens. We think we have tried to gain knowledge through argument, but in reality, the argument was inadequate. If we encounter frustration in argumentation, we should step back to see whether one party or the other in the dialogue has resorted to the use of pseudo-argument or whether we have failed to identify and address a more basic unexamined assumption. If we think presuppositionally, we can and should come to agreement. If we are knowledgeable about the kinds and uses of informal fallacies, we will avoid needless frustration and the advancement of skepticism. What follows is a summary of some of the most prevalent informal fallacies.

Appeal to fear is the use of threat to persuade to action. It succeeds where one fears losing a secondary good over a primary good. The appeal to fear was used against Socrates unsuccessfully. They threatened "stop doing philosophy, or face death." Socrates chose intellectual life (the primary good) over his physical life (a secondary good).

Appeal to pity is the abuse of the listener's disposition to compassion. It succeeds where the good of the recipient is not kept clearly in mind. It is often used to avoid responsibility where hardship is necessary.

A *straw man* argues against a misrepresentation of a position rather than the real position. Honesty and care are necessary to avoid the use of the straw man.

The *appeal to authority* appeals to someone as an authority where he or she is not an authority. This is often used where there is insufficient respect for the authority of reason.

An *ad hominem* attack speaks against the person rather than against what the person said. It is a personal attack often used when we don't have a counterargument.

The *ad populum* relies on the tendency of people to believe or go along with what is commonly accepted or done. It succeeds against those who find safety in numbers, custom, or the establishment.

Begging the question assumes to be true what one claims to be proving to be true. It is often used when a person is not aware of his or her assumptions.

A *red herring* is sidetracking the argument by bringing in what is irrelevant. Often based on associative thinking and taking things out of the original context.

The *appeal to ignorance* assumes a belief to be true if it has not been disproven. It sometimes involves an appeal to the unknown through the use of undefinable terms.

The *post hoc ergo proptor hoc* (*post hoc*), which means "after this, therefore because of this," is faulty causal reasoning based on insufficient observation or analysis.

A *hasty generalization* makes a general statement based on insufficient observation. This fallacy is often involved in stereotyping.

A *complex question* is a question that assumes more than the listener is ready to assent to; also known as the loaded question.

RATIONAL PRESUPPOSITIONALISM VS. RATIONALISM AND EMPIRICISM[2]

Rationalism and Empiricism have both led to skepticism. Rationalism has assumed that reason is a source of truth, and it has first used reason constructively rather than critically to examine basic assumptions. Empiricism has assumed that all knowledge is through sense experience, failing to recognize that experience is interpreted in light of basic assumptions that are non-empirical. Applying Rational Presuppositionalism, that we ought to think of the less basic in light of the more basic, will help us to avoid the skepticism resulting from Rationalism and Empiricism.

Rationalism

Exalted claims have been made in the name of reason, provoked in part by internecine wars, abuses, and superstitions in the name of religion. The Enlightenment affirmed the sufficiency of reason and experience to guide all human affairs. God's supernatural actions in the world were removed from providence first by deists—Hume (*On Miracles*),[3] and then by Kant (*Religion within the Bounds of Reason*

---

2. The paragraphs on Rationalism and Empiricism in this section are quoted from Gangadean, *Philosophical Foundation*, 26-27, 38-39.

3. David Hume, Enquiries Concerning Human Understanding, 3rd ed. (New York: Oxford University Press, 1975), 127. (See Section X, "Of Miracles.") "Upon the whole, then, it appears that no testimony for any kind of miracle has ever amounted to a probability, much less to a proof; and that, even supposing it amounted to a proof, it would be opposed by another proof; derived from the very nature of the fact, which it would endeavor to establish. It is experience only which gives authority to human testimony; and it is the same experience which assures us of the laws of nature. When, therefore, these two kinds of experience are contrary, we have nothing to do but to substract the one from the other, and embrace an opinion, either on one side or the other, with that assurance which arises from the remainder. But according to the principle here explained, this substraction, with regard to all popular religions, amounts to an entire annihilation; and therefore, we may establish

Alone), and later from creation by Darwin's theory of evolution and by contemporary naturalistic cosmologies. As the naturalist worldview unfolded, its excesses and superstitions were seen, and its pretensions to neutrality and morality were exposed. It appeared too that claims made in the name of reason had their dehumanizing limitations. The idol of reason was then dethroned and became subject to abuse and degradation. Over and against contemporary malaise, directionlessness, and nihilism, there is a resurgence of religion, and with it a recurrence of conflicts and wars in the name of religion. Are we forever to be caught in this bi-polar mindset, between faith and reason, between fideism and skepticism, between the right and the left?

There is a common failure to use reason on both sides of the dispute—one in the name of reason, the other in the name of God. Both rationalists and fideists failed to address the origin and significance of natural evil in light of the clarity of general revelation. In addition, fideists failed to address the nature and relation of moral and natural evil from special revelation. Given this common failure as human beings, it is ironic how each side has opposed the other, except that fideists had more opportunity to understand moral and natural evil based on scripture. Neither side can speak to the other of this common failure, so the opposition goes on. But no one is obligated to take sides in this futile dispute. No one is obligated to choose between reason without God or God without reason. A deeper sense of reason as the logos[4] in human nature, and a deeper use of reason in light of clarity, would shatter the pretensions on both sides and get us past the dangers of competing idolatries.

---

as a maxim, that no human testimony can have such force as to prove a miracle, and make it a just foundation for any such system of religion." Hume's criticism of course would not hold if miracles were not the foundation, but played a different role in one's system.

4. Kelly Fitzsimmons Burton, *Retrieving Knowledge: A Socratic Response to Skepticism* (Phoenix: Public Philosophy Press, 2018), 307-312. The prologue to the Gospel of John provides a response to the philosophical quest for the logos in Greek thought. Burton provides a commentary on the seven-fold doctrine of the logos outlined by Surrendra Gangadean, *The Word of God: The Logos is Truth* (Phoenix: Logos Papers Press, 2016), Logos Paper No. 30. See: https://thelogospapers.com

Empiricism

Empiricism is the epistemological view that all knowledge arises from sense experience. Radical empiricism goes beyond sense experience to affirm inner or religious experience grounded in intuition. Empiricism begins with common sense realism. Proof is by seeing and touching. It has been articulated and developed in the British empiricist tradition and has been assumed in much of contemporary analytical philosophy.[5] It has been applied to meaning as well: the meaning of a statement is its method of verification. If there is no empirical way to verify the truth of a statement, that statement is considered meaningless. Empiricism has increasingly been assumed in the natural sciences, and natural science is becoming the stronghold of empiricism. It professes to be the only true source of knowledge, publicly verifiable, and, therefore, authoritative for all. It is validated by its recurrent technological miracles, and it is in turn richly endowed by public grants for research and development.

Science generally, and empiricism particularly, have shown themselves to be vulnerable in a variety of ways. Far from knowing that all knowledge is from sense experience, it may be argued that some knowledge is not from sense experience (for example, there are no square-circles) or that there is no knowledge from sense experience (pure data of sense experience is not meaningful without interpretation). We do not know the reality of an external world from sense experience (as has been observed by Berkeley), or the reality of mind and causality (argued by Hume) or the reality of substance and identity/unity (the position held by Kant). By means of the senses, we do not know there are essences, or universals, or permanence, or concepts, only particulars and momentary sense impressions. Nominalism, skepticism, and legal positivism have been recurrent in ancient, medieval, and modern philosophy when the senses have become the sole source of knowledge. The antinomy of permanence and change has recurred in the East as well, between Madhyamika Buddhism and *Advaita* Vedanta. Scientific knowledge is based on observation and limited by observation. It relies on induction to go from the observed

---

5. Burton, *Retrieving* Knowledge, 201-272. Burton provides an intellectual history of philosophy in the 20th century, noting the effects of empiricism on the analytic, continental, and pragmatic schools of philosophy.

to the unobserved. Induction assumes uniformity of nature. The past and the future are like the present. The forces now operating have always operated and in essentially the same magnitude. Extended further, how things now operate is said to explain how things originate. Observation can falsify general statements. It cannot verify them. Observation cannot disconfirm the existence of non-physical realities without assuming methodological naturalism—that all phenomena can be explained in natural terms. This in turn assumes metaphysical naturalism, that all of reality is natural, that nothing is supernatural.

Given these assumptions, all distinctions can and must be reduced to simpler, natural terms. Mind must be reduced to brain, biology to chemistry, chemistry to physics, and physics to geometry and to mathematics—Pythagoras claimed that numbers are things and things are numbers. Within reductionistic explanation, as anomalies multiply, a paradigm shift may occur, but the project goes on. In reductionism, there is no logical or ontological gap between mind and brain, between non-physical mental images and physical neural impulses. There is only the project of empiricism itself, with the promissory note—some day it will be explained, naturalistically, by more observation. Science assumes induction and reduction; it assumes uniformity and naturalism, none of which are based on nor can be based on observation. By transgressing its stated boundaries, it advocates a dogmatic naturalistic interpretation of the world. With good reason, in postmodern consciousness, the world constructed by science is no longer being privileged.

Rational Presuppositionalism

Rational Presuppositionalism (RP) is an epistemological method used to settle philosophical disputes by critically analyzing assumptions for meaning. It applies reason as a test for meaning to what is presupposed in a dispute.

RP affirms that some things are clear. The basic things are clear. The basic things about God and man and good and evil are clear to reason. RP is an answer to skepticism and fideism. It is an alternative to Rationalism and to Empiricism, both of which make uncritically held assumptions.

Thinking is presuppositional. We think of the less basic in light of the more basic. We think of truth in light of meaning, experience in light of basic belief, conclusions in light of premises, and the finite and temporal in light of the infinite and eternal. If we understand what is more basic, we can understand what is less basic; if we agree on what is more basic, we can agree on what is less basic.

RP seeks to avoid needless disputes by examining if there is agreement on what is more basic. It seeks to avoid straining at gnats while swallowing camels. It looks at both the objective and the subjective aspects of knowledge and dialogue. Dialogue presupposes a commitment to reason along with an understanding of the nature of reason.

Having knowledge presupposes a concern to know, which presupposes integrity as a concern for consistency, both theoretically and personally. If there is commitment to reason, with integrity, disputes can be settled.[6]

RP is opposed to Rationalism. The psychologically self-evident is not the logically self-evident. Rationalism has used reason constructively without first using it critically. Mere incoherence between beliefs does not determine which belief should be rejected; a set of beliefs is not the same as a system of beliefs. Reason in itself is purely formal; it does not supply the content of thought. Reason in itself is abstract; it does not get to existence. Reason is first used as a test for meaning, not as a source of truth. There can be more than one logically possible world. Reason is used to test the assumptions of each.

RP is opposed to Empiricism. Ordinary experience, or common sense, assumes that appearance is reality. Analysis of perception shows the mental image is not identical to its cause. The cause of what is seen could be one's own mind. Or, the cause of what is seen could be another mind. Special outward experience (miracles) can be interpreted in many ways. Special inward experiences (mystical states) can be interpreted in many ways. Science must use non-empirical assumptions to interpret data in order to arrive at facts. No experience is meaningful without interpretation; reason is used to interpret and to test interpretations for meaning.

---

6. Parts of this section have been quoted from Gangadean, *Philosophical Foundation*.

CONCLUDING REMARKS ON SKEPTICISM

Skepticism is rooted in uncritically held assumptions. Since we think of what is less basic in light of what is more basic, agreement on the less basic will not be reached unless there is agreement on what is more basic. And, if there is clarity anywhere that will overcome skepticism, it will be clarity in regard to what is basic. So, we must identify what is basic and how what is basic is clear (recall the problem of integrity, i.e., willingness to examine one's basic beliefs, and suffering).

What is basic is basic in relation to thought. What is most basic in relation to thought is what makes thought possible, and what is our most basic thought. What is necessary for thought are the laws of thought, reason. And what is necessary for understanding and explaining change is causality. All thought is about being (or some quality, state, activity, or relation of being). So, the concept of being is also basic, and since being changes, what is necessary to understand and/ or to explain change, is causality. Lastly, putting being and change together in regard to coming into being requires that being either existed always or came into being. Being is either eternal or temporal. So, the concepts of temporal and eternal (along with finite and infinite) are basic and apply to all being. What is basic in thinking is reason, being, cause, and kind of being (eternal and temporal, and its corollaries of infinite and eternal).

If there is agreement on these basics, then there will be agreement on what is less basic. Disagreement about the basics will take the form of directly denying the existence of reason, cause, being, etc., or indirectly denying their existence by denying their nature, for example, by claiming that reason does not apply to being, or that causality does not apply to being. Direct or indirect denial of the existence of what is basic makes thought impossible. In this way, what is basic, or what is necessary for thought is clear. In this sense, the basics are the transcendentals, the necessary condition for the possibility of thought. Denial of the basics, or transcendentals, is the denial of thought. Although one may continue to speak while denying what is basic, one's words are emptied of meaning and become meaninglessness.

Chapter 2

THE TRANSCENDENTALS

SKEPTICISM IS ROOTED IN UNCRITICALLY held assumptions. If skepticism is to be rooted out, we must critically examine our assumptions. The willingness to critically examine assumptions is a matter of integrity. With which assumptions are we to begin? We are to begin with our most basic assumptions, with the conditions necessary for the possibility of thought itself. That is, the laws of thought.

Thought must be distinguished from what is not thought, such as feeling, sensation, perception, and behavior. And it must be distinguished as well from the thinker and the object of thought, which is being or some aspect of being. Thought begins with the formation of concepts, comes to its first complete expression in judgment, which joins or separates concepts, and has its fullest expression in argument, in which two (or more) judgments are used to logically support a conclusion. These things may appear to be too simple to be worth saying, but often enough, the problem of skepticism and disputes begins here.

Since thought is about being, we must examine the concept of being in contrast to thought, and to becoming, and to non-being. This in turn will require distinguishing changing from unchanging being and examining causality as the necessary cause for change and the explanation of change. Here Aristotle's treatment of causality, as well as Hume's and Kant's, as well as views of causality in quantum physics come to mind. What is most basic in thinking is first reason, as the laws of thought, then being, as that which thought is about, then distinction in being between what comes into being (the temporal) and what does not come into being (the eternal), and that by which coming into being or change occurs—causality.

REASON

The purpose of these remarks is to clarify what is meant by reason, to show its significance, and to remove some of the common obstacles to its use. Reason is central in many important issues that have been discussed for a long time, issues such as reason and faith, reason and experience, skepticism and certainty, meaning and truth, reason and subjectivity (individualism), truth and love (reason and emotions), intellect and will, common ground in discussion, relation of general and special revelation, clarity of revelation and moral accountability, and the limits of reason (incomprehensibility, mysticism, and paradox). There is, therefore, need to be precise in understanding what is meant by reason and its uses before trying to understand any of these issues.

Reason in Itself

Reason is the laws of thought. Just as physics and biology have laws that make these aspects of being possible, so thought is made possible by its laws, reason. When reason is violated, thought ceases. What is uttered is no longer meaningful; that is, it cannot be thought and, therefore, is no longer possibly true or false. It is necessarily false or impossible. A statement is clear when its contradiction is, upon critical examination, seen to be logically impossible or meaningless because it violates a law of thought or reason. Since clarity, and with it, inexcusability, depends on reason, we must be clear about the nature and limits of reason.

Reason can be defined in itself, in its use, and (as it exists) in us. In itself, reason consists of three laws: the law of identity, the law of non-contradiction, and the law of excluded middle. The law of identity is that a thing is what it is; a is a; rock is rock; fish is fish; later, this will be applied to distinguishing being and non-being, true and not true (false), a thing and a thought, a relation, quality, substance, mind and brain, and more. Two things are identical if they have the same set of properties. The law of identity is used in forming all concepts in which one (kind of) thing is identified and distinguished from all else: rock and non-rock, fish and non-fish, etc.

The law of non-contradiction is that a thing cannot be both a and *non-a*, at the same time and in the same respect. Something cannot be both square and not square, at the same time and in the same respect. Or a statement cannot be both true and not true, at the same time and in the same respect. A thing may be both blue and not blue in the same respect at different times or be both blue and not blue in differ-ent respects (say, to different perceivers) at the same time. As applied to statements, contradictory statements cannot both be true, and they cannot both be false. If one is true, the other must be false, and vice versa. "Some S is P" and "No S is P," or "Some apples are red" and "No apples are red" are contradictories and cannot both be true and cannot both be false. This is a paradigm of clarity and will be used in proving what is clear about what is basic.

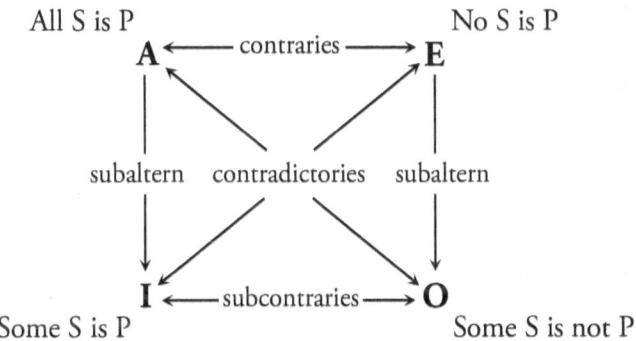

The law of excluded middle is that a thing is either *a* or *non-a*; there is no third. A being is either eternal (without beginning) or non-eternal (temporal—with beginning). A statement is either true or not true (false). A being is either extended (material) or non-extended (spirit). A (material) being is either black or non-black (not black or white). There is no third alternative. A thing may be both black and non-black, but not at the same time and in the same respect. And a thing may be neither black nor non-black because it does not belong to the category of things that have color. Still, it is either in a category capable of color or incapable of color. Attention must be given to dis-tinctions between categories and within categories to avoid confusion and cavalier objections to the validity of the law of excluded middle.

These laws are constantly being used wherever anyone is thinking at all. They are so basic we are often not aware of using them. People think, but they do not think about thinking, just as they breathe, but do not think about breathing. We do not consider that there are laws of thought, let alone try to name and describe the laws or show how they apply to understanding the meaning of what is said. We say things, but do not think deeply about the meaning of what we say. For this reason, there are many unexamined and uncritically held assumptions from which unending disputes arise.

Reason in Its Use

We continue to define reason by now considering reason in its use. We can identify four uses of reason. Reason is used to form concepts, judgments, and arguments, the forms of all thought. Reason is used critically to test for meaning. Reason is used to interpret experience in light of one's basic beliefs. And reason is used to construct a world and life view. We can call these the formative, critical, interpretive, and constructive uses of reason. I will examine each of these uses of reason and their relation to each other. It needs to be said here, and must be repeated many times, that a failure in the use of reason is not a failure in reason itself. This is why the distinction is being made between reason and reason in its use. It is a straw man argument to say reason itself fails when the failure is in the use of reason.

The *first* use of reason is its formative use. It is used to form concepts, judgments, and arguments, which are the forms of all thought. The first act of reason is the forming of a concept. In a concept, the mind grasps the essence of a thing. The essence of a thing is the quality or set of qualities that all members of a class have, that they always have, and which distinguishes that class from all other things. This applies to individual beings as well as to the qualities, states, relations, and activities of beings. It applies to classes with one or more members. For example, the qualities that all humans have, that they always have, and which distinguish them from all non-humans are the qualities of being rational and animal. By rational is meant the capacity to reason, however underdeveloped, hindered, or neglected its use may be. A concept is universal in that it applies to all members of a class, and it is the same in all rational beings having the concept. We agree that past, color, height, weight, and age are not part of the concept "human," because we do not all have the same height, nor does a person always have the same height.

A concept, the first act of reason, must be distinguished from an image, which is through the use of the senses. Images are not universal, but differ from one member of a class to another and differ also in each perceiver. A concept is not a feeling (sadness) or sensation (pain). A concept is not orderly behavior, since there can be orderly response without thought or even perception (activities governed by the autonomic nervous system).

A concept is expressed by a conceptual sign, ordinarily, a word or term (a group of words). Each time a word is uttered, a concept is being expressed. For example, the words "man," "table," "star," "blue," "sad," "time," and "running," express concepts in which (the essence) of "man" is distinguished from what is not "man," "table" from what is not "table," etc. Words are conventional signs used to express concepts and are subject to the plurality of convention. A word may be ambiguous and used to express more than one concept. For example, "ring" as a sound, and "ring" as a band on one's finger, and "ring" as in a ring of thieves. At the same time, a concept may be expressed by several words such as "mind," "soul," "spirit," "self," and "consciousness," express that in us which is aware. Besides ordinary ambiguity, words have philosophical ambiguity. Though Buddhists, materialists, and theists may agree on the reference of "man" (the members that belong to the class), they disagree on the sense of the term, each having a different metaphysical framework about the nature of reality in which the concept "man" is embedded. So, unexamined assumptions about the meaning of terms often contribute to disputes which remain unresolved until the assumptions are examined.

The second formative use of reason builds on its first use. Reason is used to form judgments, in which concepts are joined by affirmation or separated by negation. For example, "all men are mortal" and "some men are not wise." While concepts are neither true nor false (they may be well formed or not well formed with respect to having meaning). Judgments are judged as either true or false. By reason, a judgment cannot be both true and false, at the same time and in the same respect. It simply is not possible for the mind to think this, just as one cannot both think and not think at the same time and in the same respect. So, "some is eternal" and "none is eternal" cannot both be true and cannot both be false. And, as judgments, they cannot be neither true nor false. If "none is eternal" cannot be true, "some is eternal" must be true.

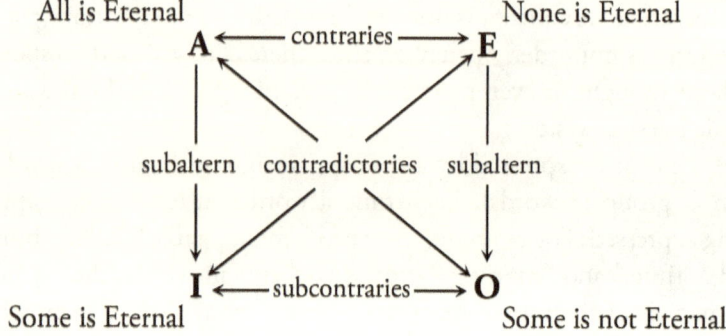

All is Eternal   None is Eternal

A ←—— contraries ——→ E

subaltern   contradictories   subaltern

I ←— subcontraries —→ O

Some is Eternal   Some is not Eternal

Most, if not all, disputes will come down to whether reason is being violated in forming judgments, or whether one is committed to the use of reason in forming judgments, or whether what appears to be a judgment is not, in reality, a judgment. If this use of reason, which is so basic, is not agreed upon, there cannot be agreement on anything else. What remains is non-cognitivist expression of feeling or operation of power, not anything that is possibly true or false.

The third formative use of reason builds on the first and second use. Here reason is used to form arguments. An argument uses premises (judgments) to logically support a conclusion (the point one is trying to make). Arguments may be complex and long (an entire book may constitute an argument) or simple and short (two premises and a conclusion). For example: All men are mortal (premise); Socrates is a man (premise); Therefore, Socrates is mortal (conclusion). Or: If it rains, then the ground is wet (premise); the ground is wet (premise); Therefore, it has rained (conclusion). The second argument is not valid. Still, it is an argument. An argument becomes necessary whenever one asserts a judgment, and one is asked why that judgment should be believed. Premises can be questioned as well, and this may regress until one carries out a *reductio ad absurdum* argument, in which the contradiction of what is asserted is seen as false because it is logically impossible. Arguments are judged as valid if the premises logically support the conclusion and sound if they are valid and the premises are true. A rational person will agree with the conclusion of a sound argument. If one does not agree, it is because one is not engaged in, or committed to, the use of reason. Arguments are the third and last of the formative use of reason. Arguments are necessary to support one's judgment and having supported one's judgment, there is nothing more to be said.

Reason is so inherent and basic in the thinking process that we cannot not be rational and still have a thought. Even false judgments require the use of reason in forming the concepts that make up the (false) judgment. Relativists, skeptics, and postmodernists who doubt or question reason are still using reason. Mystics, too, if their utterances have any cognitive meaning so as to be possibly true or false, must use reason, even when the utterance is a paradox wrapped in a metaphor. One may question rationalism, whether abstract or empirical, as in Plato or Aristotle, Descartes or Hume, or as synthesized in Kant, but one cannot question reason itself. For in questioning, one is using concepts, judgments, and arguments, which are formed by reason.

The *second* use of reason is the critical use of reason. Reason is used as a test for meaning. Meaning is more basic than truth. One must understand what a judgment means before one can judge it to be true or false. If I say (some) apples are red, since the meaning is easily understood, one can judge it, in this case, to be true. If I say, "bliks are grue," one is puzzled, since the meaning of "bliks" and "grue" is unknown until I specify what they mean. If I say "bliks are non-bliks," I can know this cannot be true, whatever the meaning of "bliks" may be because it violates the law of identity, which says *a* is *a*; *a* is not *non-a*, whatever "a" may be. To say "bliks are non-bliks" is meaningless and cannot be thought. It cannot be true and is necessarily false, not merely false. In this sense, reason is first a test for meaning, and secondly a test for falsehood, when there is no meaning. Any utterance which violates a law of reason, if it is self-contradictory upon analysis of the concepts, is meaningless and necessarily false.

Sometimes a judgment is meaningless because the meaning of its terms cannot be specified so as to distinguish it from its opposite or complement. Anaximander said, "all is *Apeiron*" (indeterminate). But if the ultimate category of being has no specific quality which distinguishes it from non-being, then it has no meaning. So too in the utterance "God is love." If this is qualified in response to the problem of evil, so as to die the death of a thousand qualifications, then the meaning is lost, and it cannot be true. Anything is compatible with the unknown. Often in disputes, key terms are ambiguated or emptied of meaning. The critical use of reason seeks to clarify the meaning of terms and judgments and analyze what is being said for coherence of meaning. When the analysis of meaning is complete, it becomes clear whether or not a law of reason is being violated. It is at this most basic level of meaning that some things are clear.

The popular view that contrasts faith and reason does not take into account this basic sense of reason. Wherever there is meaning, there is the use of reason. Since what has no meaning cannot be believed to be true, belief or faith cannot be separated from reason. This can be summed up by saying faith is to reason as truth is to meaning. As understanding of meaning increases, so faith increases. And as understanding of meaning is tested, so faith is tested. The critical use of reason is necessary in order to test and to increase one's understanding of the meaning of what is believed. One cannot speak against the use of reason, in understanding belief, without emptying belief of meaning.

The *third* use of reason is its interpretive use. Reason is used to interpret, or give meaning to, experience in light of one's basic beliefs. There is a distinction between the pure data of experience, and the meaning given to the data through interpretation. No experience is meaningful without interpretation. "There is a table before me" is different from "there appears to be a table before me," which is still different from "there is a brown color patch in my visual field," etc. The earth appears flat. The sun appears to rise. Appearance depends on the condition of the perceiver. Appearance is not reality; and the relation between the two is not known by experience, which give mere appearance only. The cause of what appears is explained in terms of what kind of causal factors are possible given one's basic belief.

Fourth and last, is the constructive use of reason.[1] Reason is used to construct a coherent world and life view.[2] In man's basic need for

---

1. The section on the fourth use of reason, and reason in us, is quoted from Gangadean, *Philosophical Foundation*, 13-15.

2. Some philosophers, more than others, engage in developing systematically the implications of their basic beliefs (Plato, Spinoza, Hegel). These are often taken as exemplary users of reason, and their teachings as "the deliverances of reason." But the constructive use of reason is not the critical use of reason, especially at the level of basic belief. Plato did not

meaning, every dimension of life gets connected. In each worldview, some things must be said, and some things cannot be said, given the requirements of reason for system and coherence. The constructive use of reason is not the critical use of reason, but its claims are often passed off as "the deliverance of reason."[3] This claim of the constructive use of reason, made in the name of reason, is what is often called rationalism. In rejecting the pretensions made in the name of reason, many uncritically denounce reason generally and indiscriminately, both in itself and in its other uses. The limits of reason within a given system are not to be identified with the limits of reason per se. Reason in itself must be distinguished from reason in its (several) uses and from reason in us.

Reason in Us

Reason in us is natural, ontological, transcendental, and fundamental. Reason as the laws of thought in us is natural, not conventional. It is universal, the same in all who think. There is not a Greek and a non-Greek rationality; there is not a male and a female rationality; there is not an old and a young, or a rich and a poor rationality, although these have become lines of division among human beings. Reason, as the laws of thought in us, is the common ground for all who think. It is the common ground between theists and non-theists, even when different claims are being made about reason based on different views of reality and human nature. To make any claim using concepts, judgments, and arguments is to use reason. No one professes to make a claim which is both true and not true, at the same time and in the same respect. One cannot deny that reason is the common ground and yet hold that contradictory statements cannot both be true. That

---

analyze critically his assumptions that the soul and matter are eternal. The system is only as sound as the assumptions. If matter and the soul are not eternal, then the system as a system is fundamentally flawed. A flawed system does not negate passion and brilliance in so much as the particulars within the system.

3. Plato, *Complete Works*, ed. John M. Cooper and D.S. Hutchinson (Indianapolis, IN: Hackett Publishing Company, 1997), "Republic," 509. Here the first principle of being, the *principium essendi*, coincides with the first principle of knowledge, the *principium cognoscendi*. This is implicit in saying thought is about being. Plato affirmed that the light which is higher than the sun (illustrated in the Allegory of the Cave) is both the source of being and the source of the intelligibility of being.

would be to affirm the law of non-contradiction, a law of reason, as common ground, while denying reason is the common ground.

Reason is ontological. It applies to being as well as to thought. There are no square-circles. This is known by reason alone. What is logically impossible is ontologically impossible.[4] There is no being from non-being; there is no uncaused event. Reason applies to all being, to the highest being, to God's being. God is not both *a* and *non-a*. God is not both eternal and non-eternal, at the same time and in the same respect. As an aspect of God's being, reason is eternal, not created. The laws of nature in theism are created; the laws of reason are not created, but that by which creation comes to be. Miracles may be acts of God which stand above, apart from, or against the laws of nature, since these are created laws, but miracles cannot be against reason. If water is changed into wine, it is not both water and not water (that is to say, wine) at the same time. Claims made by science or by religion or by philosophy which go against reason are unwarranted and cannot stand.

Reason is transcendental. It is authoritative. It stands above all thinking and makes thinking possible. It cannot be questioned for it makes questioning possible. It is self-attesting. It testifies to itself and cannot be testified to by another. It is the highest authority in the realm of human knowledge. The deliverances of prophets, poets, philosophers, and physicists must be in accord with reason. Prophets must speak in the name of God, consistent with what is clear about God from creation. The poet's intuition is not infallible in a morally fallible world. Philosophers cannot deny reason and make any affirmation about being. So too physicists cannot deny reason in affirming uncaused events in the origin of the universe or in quantum physics.

Reason is fundamental. It is fundamental to other aspects of human personality. Beliefs direct desires and together they both move the will. We desire what we believe is the good and act to achieve what we desire. The apparent conflict between belief and desire, and belief and the will, are to be explained by inconsistencies and insufficiencies in understanding—lacks which are culpable or inexcusable in light of

---

4. In the prologue to his *Gospel*, John wrote: "All things were made by him" (the Logos). He goes on to say, "In him (the Logos) was life; and the life was the light of men." Many have identified this light with reason, and as such, the highest authority, which is self-attesting.

clarity. Reason is fundamental also in that its use is the source of man's greatest happiness and its disuse is the source of man's deepest misery. By reason we understand the meaning of things. Meaning absorbs and satisfies our attention. We are willing to die to preserve what gives life meaning. The lack of meaning leaves us empty and bored. We seek to escape the emptiness and boredom through excess, which never satisfies, or through death, by suicide.

Reason, as the source of meaning, is what is most basic. There will be need to return often to what is briefly sketched here. Disputes are to be resolved by agreeing on what is more basic, and reason is most basic. Reason does not persuade and should not be expected to persuade. Reason clarifies and makes us more aware. In clarifying, it compels greater consistency; it moves us one way or the other. It is the light which shines in the darkness, and which cannot be withstood by the darkness. There is a choice, in the end. The choice is between reason and no reason, between meaning and no meaning, between light and darkness, between life and death.

BEING

Being and Non-Being

In this section, we will explore the relation of being and non-being using the following concepts: creation *ex nihilo*; unmanifest being (energy); invisible being (spirit); imaginary being (fictional); *a* from *non-a* (child/parents); the void (medium of waves), and philosophical examples including the naked singularity, Thales and change, Buddhism, and Hegel.

Creation *ex nihilo* is creation of being out of no preexisting material. It is creation from nothing. This has been thought impossible because it appears to be being coming into existence from non-being, and as such it would be also an uncaused event. However, creation *ex nihilo* asserts the eternally existing God as the source of being and the act of God as the cause of being coming into existence.

Non-being is not the same as unmanifest being such as energy. Because something cannot be seen with ordinary sense perception does not mean it does not or cannot exist.

Non-being is not the same as invisible being such as spirit. Because something cannot be detected in principle by scientific means does not mean it is non-being. Because something is non-physical does not mean it is non-being.

Non-being is not the same as imaginary being. We can speak of the latter, but not of the former. There are all kinds of imaginary beings having a host of recognizable qualities. Non-being cannot be spoken of because it lacks all properties.

Non-being is not the same as *non-a*. While being from non-being has the logical form of *a* from *non-a*, the latter is possible while the former is not. Both *a* and *non-a* are categories of being. Non-being is not a category of being. To say *a* is not *non-a* is to distinguish the two; it is not to exclude or oppose the two, as, for example, parent and non-parent (child), and infinite and finite.

Non-being is not the same as space or the void. Space might be considered as a medium of energy through which electromagnetic waves move. If space is taken to mean the absence of all energy, then space would be non-being.

Sometimes the notion of non-being is brought in under the guise of unknowable being, or being devoid of all attributes, or being possessing all attributes. Nirguna Brahman is attributeless being. The One of Plotinus is beyond all name, possessing fullness of being, of which nothing can be said. A naked singularity, or the infinitely small, or all of space as a true vacuum is indistinguishable from non-being. Anaximander's indeterminate has no particular quality. Heraclitus' flux, becoming without being, Buddhist first truth that all is impermanent, require close attention to see if what is meant is different from non-being. Hegel seems to say that being interacts with non-being to give rise to becoming.

Existentialism, in affirming that existence precedes essence, seems to suggest there can be essenceless being. If so, how is this different from non-being? The reader is here being alerted to distinguish being from non-being in basic beliefs.

Being and Aspect of Being

Aspects of being can be states (happy), relations (near), properties (red), or activities (thinking) of beings. Aspects of being are not to be identified with being as if they are things which exist in themselves rather than in being. Aristotle thought Plato fell into this error in his attempt to establish knowledge by having a permanent object existing apart from this changing world. There has been a long dispute, which is still continuing on, whether laws, numbers, properties, and propositions exist in themselves. For now, at least, it can be said that these are not found in ordinary experience to exist in themselves however else the kind and necessity of their existence may be accounted for.

There are examples of problematic assertions which confuse being and aspect of being. Could laws have created the world or are laws constitutive of what is created? Could the good be the source of being or is the good what is achieved by the activity of beings? Is history reason expressing itself in time or is a rational plan as the result of the activity of a being coming to expression in history? Does time exist in itself prior to and apart from things or is time a relation among things? Is the self a bundle of impressions or are impressions the result of the activity of the self in response to stimuli? In these examples, the concept of being is obscured by collapsing the distinction between being and aspect of being. Sometimes a being is treated as an aspect of being, and sometimes an aspect of being is treated as a being. If being is without aspects, then being is indistinguishable from non-being; and if aspects are without being, then they are aspects of non-being, neither of which is intelligible.

Being and Thought

Thoughts are not beings, but the product of thinking; and beings are not thoughts. Philosophical idealism corrects naive realism, but over-extends itself.

Common sense takes appearance for reality. It takes our thought for being. Upon examination, this naive realism collapses. The world appears flat, but is not flat. The water of the ocean appears blue, but is not blue. Light waves themselves, if such exist, are not conceived as having color. So, all we see belongs to appearance, to our thought, not to reality itself. All that we are immediately aware of through sense perception are sense data, which exists in the perceiver and not the external world. When being is identified with thought we lose being.

Philosophical idealism also takes appearance for reality. It takes being to be thought. To be is to be perceived, according to Berkeley. Since we can never get beyond our thoughts, we have no warrant for thinking there is a reality beyond thought. The cause of what is seen is one's own mind or some other mind. There is not a mind-independent physical table that is the cause of the table that is seen. Thought and being are one and the same. While Kantian and postmodern idealism differ from classical idealism in the West or East, all idealism agrees that either there is no reality beyond thought or this reality is unknowable. So again, when being is identified with thought we lose being.

Being and Substance

Substance is defined as that which exists in itself and not in another (in contrast to aspects of being); being without the form of a particular being; that out of which a being is formed; not made up of anything else; that in which qualities inhere. Substance is not a mode or dimension. There are two kinds of substances: matter and spirit. Matter is extended and non-conscious; spirit is non-extended and conscious.

The concept of substance is somewhat elusive, but necessary. In the history of philosophy and of thought in general, it has been commonly recognized that there are two substances, matter and spirit. Substance is elusive in that it is other than the qualities which are said to inhere in it, yet not much can be said of it except that these qualities inhere in it. It is sometimes said that it is something we know not what. This is true of material as well as non-material substance.

Rocks, trees, and stars are of material substance, equally. Souls, angels, and God are spirit, or are of spiritual substance, equally. The former all have spatial qualities and are non-conscious; the latter all lack spatial qualities and are conscious. So, it is not true that they are each a total unknown. And the distinguishing qualities cannot be collapsed. Conscious is not the same as non-conscious; the extended is not the same as the non-extended. Since these qualities are exhaustive and exclusive, there are two and only two substances. Questions of how they can be in relation if so different, and whether both are equally independent of each other remain. These will be taken up when considering the question of what is eternal.

Being and A Being

A being is substance of a particular form (or essence) that has been individuated. A being has functional unity. While substance has being and qualities have being, neither substance nor qualities are found to exist except in individual beings, or in groups made up of individual beings, or groups made up of groups of individual beings. Thus, the individual being is the fundamental unit of reality. Nothing exists apart from individuals. Being cannot be spoken of apart from individual beings. To say a being has functional unity is to say a being is a unity of substance and qualities, and that neither substance nor qualities has function apart from a being.

Being and Essence

If we think and speak of being, we have to think and speak of essences. The essence of a class of beings is the set of qualities that all members have, that they always have, and which distinguish them from non-members. An individual being has an essence that is general for a class, and particular, for itself only.

Every individual has an essence, and every class has an essence that distinguishes it from other individuals and classes. The concept of a being or class of beings grasps the essence of that being or class. Terms are used to express concepts and so express the essence grasped by the concept.

Beside essential qualities there are non-essential qualities, or what are called accidental qualities. These are qualities which not all members of a class possess, or which an individual does not always possess (for example, age for the class of human beings or for a particular human being).

We, therefore, cannot think of a being, which is fundamental to the concept of being, without thinking of its essence or essential qualities. Attempts to do so lead to an unknowable, which is no different from non-being. Such cannot be thought. Yet attempts to assert essenceless being is a temptation some fall into. To speak of existence preceding essence, or God beyond all qualities, or an Indeterminate source of all phenomena (Kant's *noumena*, Lao Tzu's *Tao*, Anaximander's *Apeiron*) is to appeal to the unknown which lacks all qualities of being. To think is to think of being, and to think of being is to think of essences.

Being and Unity

A thing can be "one" in more than one sense. We will consider several senses of unity. Speaking of numerical unity, a being is one and the same. "One" can mean the same essence; same nature as, such as the Father and the Son are one. "One" can mean non-dualism, where all is one without any difference.

We may consider several forms of the unity of diversity, where each thing is "one" by virtue of many (parts). Consider atoms, which have protons, electrons, and neutrons (non-living); the amoeba, which is made up of atoms and is living; animals, where there is variety in each and among all; humans, which have a body (physical) and soul (non-physical and are male and female); and the unity of persons in the Trinity. God is said to be one being, three persons, Father, Son, and Holy Spirit. In the ontological Trinity, each person is equally God, sharing the same substance and attributes. In the economical Trinity, each person is in relation to the other. The Father eternally decrees and elects; the Son is the eternal Word and redeemer; the Holy Spirit eternally preserves and applies redemption.

We may consider ethical unity, where persons are united because they share the same purpose. The good is the source of ethical unity in oneself, between persons, and between groups of persons.

The last sense of unity to consider is natural and collective unity. An example of a natural unity is the universe, which is the unity of the diversity of all that physically exists. An example of a collective unity is the university, which is the unity of the diverse disciplines that represent the cumulative knowledge of the ages.

Being and Eternal Existence

Eternal is without beginning and without end, minimally. What is eternal is independent, self-existing, self-maintaining, and self-explaining. Eternal is not aeveternal—eternal in time; eternal is timeless. Eternal is not temporal (with a beginning) or everlasting (merely without end). Whatever is eternal is also infinite. There are no unique events for an eternal being (the sun or the soul). Eternal is our most basic quality of being, logically and ontologically. There must be something eternal.

OUR MOST BASIC CONCEPT
AND MOST BASIC BELIEF

Our most basic belief is about our most basic concept. Logically, the most basic concept is that of existence. The most basic thing we can say about anything is that "it is," which is prior to any of its qualities. Existence is of two kinds: temporal (with beginning) and eternal (without beginning). Eternal existence is prior (logically and ontologically) to temporal existence. We have a precise concept (not image) of what eternal means.

Eternal is not the same as everlasting or aeveternal (in time). Disputes arise when these basic differences are not kept clearly in mind.

There are no unique events in an eternal being or process:

1. If there were an infinite amount of time, it could not be explained why a unique event did not happen before it did.
2. How can a unique event happen at all in an eternal (infinite) series?
   a. An infinite series cannot be crossed in finite time.
   b. There cannot be an infinite series, since what is infinite is indivisible.
   c. Since time is divisible, time must not be an infinite series.

Argument That There Must Be Something Eternal

There must be at least something eternal (assuming anything exists at all). The contradictory "nothing is eternal" is self-contradictory (by *reductio* argument):

1. If nothing is eternal, then all is temporal.
2. If all is temporal, then all had a beginning.
3. If all had a beginning, then all came into being.
4. If all came into being, then being would have come from non-being.

Since "being from non-being" violates the law of identity, this is impossible. Therefore, "nothing is eternal" is impossible, and "some is eternal" must be true.

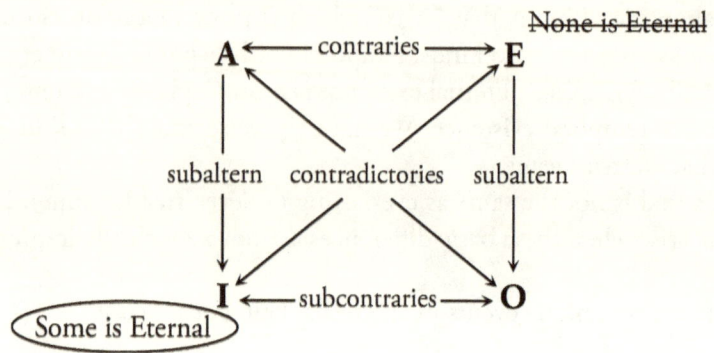

Our presupposition is the most basic belief that we use to interpret our experience. There are two presuppositions: either "all is eternal" (in some form or other) or "only some is eternal." No one is fully conscious or consistent in their presupposition; there is an admixture of both in varying degrees in each person, with one being more basic than the other.

History is reason (logos) unfolding the meaning of one's presupposition in time. Rationally, one or the other presupposition must be true (both cannot be true by the law of non-contradiction, and both cannot be false by the law of excluded middle).

Logically, all historic belief systems can be classified as "all," or "only some is eternal." "All is eternal" includes material monism, spiritual monism, dualism, pluralism, etc. (being/becoming). "Only some is eternal" includes theism (Judaism, Christianity, Islam) and deism (Creator/creation).

CAUSALITY AND UNCAUSED EVENTS

The argument against "nothing is eternal" is a *reductio ad absurdum* argument. That is to say, it is absurd or rationally unintelligible to think being came into existence from non-being. To deny being from non-being is to deny uncaused events. Some analysis may help clarify matters further.

The Epistemological Status of Belief in Causality

Belief in causality is not an empirical claim. Causality, or its absence, cannot be known by observation. There is not any indicator, and there can be no indicator of causality or the lack of causality. Belief in causality is transcendental. It is a necessary condition for the intelligibility of the world and of thought.

If there can be one uncaused event, there can be more than one uncaused event. Any or many or all events may be uncaused. There is no non-arbitrary rational way to limit the number of uncaused events. If one uncaused event is logically possible, then all events can be uncaused, and then nothing would be logically impossible.

If uncaused events were possible, it is possible there are no causal connections whatsoever between a thought or a sense impression and a cause in either the external world or in my mind. There could be no causal connection between what one person said and what the other person heard, or between one thought and another (premise and conclusion) in anyone's mind, or between intention and act in any person. As a matter of integrity, belief in causality is a necessary condition for belief in thinking and for dialogue.

Being From Non-Being and Uncaused Events

Being from non-being is not creation *ex nihilo*. In creation *ex nihilo*, God exists eternally (in contrast to nothing is eternal), and God acts to bring the world into existence. The world coming into existence by a divine act of creation is not an uncaused event.

Being from non-being is not coming into existence by an unknown or unknowable cause (as in quantum physics). An unknown or unknowable cause is still a cause; it is not non-being.

Being from non-being is not causation by an invisible being, material or spiritual. Appeal to a singularity to explain the origin of the universe is not an uncaused event, since there are no uncaused events. An uncaused event is not the same as an uncaused being. An uncaused being is an eternal being. An event is not a being.

Being from non-being is like an atom or a sub-atomic particle or a person coming into existence from absolute non-being, without any cause whatsoever. Being from non-being is not to be understood as being caused to be by nothing or non-being as the cause. Nothing or non-being is not a cause. Caused by nothing is equivalent by obversion to not caused by anything. Not caused by anything is an uncaused event.

Is Being from Non-Being a Contradiction?

Being from non-being is said to be like *a* from *non-a*. Since *a* from *non-a* is not a contradiction (like matter from spirit or a chicken from an egg), then being from non-being is not a contradiction. In response, being from non-being is not like *a* from *non-a*. *Non-a* is still in the category of being, not non-being. Being from non-being is like *a* from neither *a* nor *non-a*, if *a* and *non-a* can be considered to encompass all categories of being. It would be like matter from neither matter nor spirit or a chicken from neither chicken nor egg.

Since being from non-being is not a contradiction like a square-circle, it is said to be not a contradiction (even if it is thought to be false and unbelievable). In response, being from non-being is not a formal contradiction stated in this form, but it implies a formal contradiction. If being from non-being were possibly true, then being would be no different from non-being. If being is no different from non-being, then being is non-being, which is a contradiction. It violates the law of identity and the law of non-contradiction: something is both *a* and *non-a*, at the same time and in the same respect.

PART II

METAPHYSICS

Chapter 3

———

ON WHAT IS ETERNAL

PROOF FOR THE EXISTENCE OF GOD[1]

PROOF ASSUMES REASON, WHICH IS the laws of thought. These are the law of identity (*a* is *a*), the law of non-contradiction (not both *a* and *non-a*), and the law of excluded middle (either *a* or *non-a*). Reason applies to being as well as thought. There are no square-circles. A statement is not both true and not true, at the same time and in the same respect.

There are no uncaused events. Being cannot come from non-being. Eternal is not temporal, and infinite is not finite. God is not both eternal and not eternal (temporal). If these basics are in place, proof is possible. Without these, thought is impossible.

By the term "God" is meant an eternal being, greater than all, therefore, Creator of all. To prove the existence of God, it is necessary to prove there must be something eternal and that only some is eternal. What is eternal would bring into existence or create what is not eternal. The proof modifies each and combines all of the historically independent arguments for the existence of God. The ontological argument shows there must be something eternal. The cosmological argument shows only some is eternal. The natural teleological argument shows special creation rather than theistic (macro)-evolution. The moral teleological argument shows that both moral and natural evil serve the good.

---

1. For a more complete exposition of the proofs for the existence of God, see Gangadean, *Philosophical Foundation*, Chapters 4-7.

THE ONTOLOGICAL ARGUMENT:
There Must Be Something Eternal

As shown in the last chapter, the proof is by the *reductio* argument: the contradictory "none is eternal" cannot be true. If none were eternal, then all would be temporal, all would have a beginning, and all would have come into being from non-being. Since being from non-being is impossible, "none is eternal" cannot be true, and its contradictory "some is eternal" must be true.

THE COSMOLOGICAL ARGUMENT:
Only Some Is Eternal

Neither matter nor the soul is eternal. What is eternal must be self-existing, self-maintaining, with no unique events in time.

Argument: If the material universe were eternal, it would be self-maintaining. The material universe is not self-maintaining. Therefore, the material universe is not eternal.

Reason for the minor premise: the material universe is not self-maintaining 1) in general, 2) in part, or 3) in whole. 1) The universe is highly differentiated in terms of hot and cold. These differences interact. The interaction continues until it reaches sameness. Sameness will remain sameness. 2) The stars are not self-maintaining. Each sun or star is finite in size, and each is giving off heat and cannot do so forever. They will burn out and, therefore, must have had a beginning. The sun and stars declare themselves to be finite and temporal. 3) The universe as a whole can be self-maintaining only if all that has been scattered can be regathered. If there is too little mass, it will not be regathered. If there is too much mass, it could not be scattered. If there is just the right amount of mass, it will neither be scattered nor regathered and so could not be in its present highly differentiated state. Recent and historic attempts to support a self-maintaining material universe have appealed to uncaused events or being from non-being to get out of the state of sameness.

It can be shown that the soul exists, in contrast to material monism, by showing that the mind is distinct from the brain and that brain activity logically cannot account for thought and perception. The property of thought (true or false) cannot be reduced to the properties of motion of atoms in the brain (fast or slow etc.). The last brain activity (the neural impulse) is not identical with the table that I see (the mental image).[2]

It can be shown that the soul's existence and separateness is not illusory, in contrast to spiritual monism, by showing that illusion cannot be in the soul or in Brahman, and that it is not part of God because what is infinite is complete in itself and is without parts.

Since the soul exists, if the soul were eternal, it would be infinite in knowledge. But it is clearly not infinite in knowledge. So, it is finite and temporal and, therefore, created.

In contrast to idealism, the cause of what I see is neither my mind nor some other mind, but outside all minds (i.e., matter). If my mind were the cause, I would have total control, and I don't; if some other mind were the cause, I would not have any control, and I do.

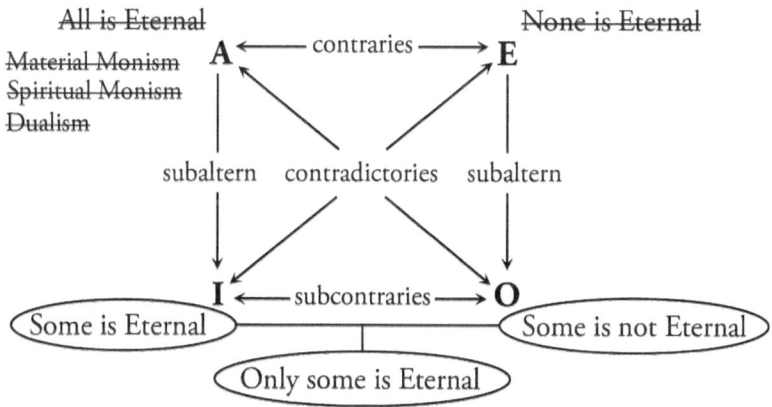

THE NATURAL TELEOLOGICAL ARGUMENT:
Order in the World Is by Special Creation, Not Theistic Evolution

The teleological argument assumes God's existence from the ontological and cosmological arguments. It does not prove the existence of an eternal Creator, but shows the manner of creation.

---

2. Gangadean, *Philosophical Foundation*, 82-86.

God, as Creator, is all powerful and all good. Since God is all powerful and all good, he could and would make a world without natural evil. If he could and would, then he must. And if he must, then he did. A world without natural evil is incompatible with theistic macroevolution in which animals devour each other and physical death for humans is part of the original condition.

In theistic evolution, the soul of man is added to an already existing living being that has evolved over millions of years. But this assumes there is a difference between the soul and the life of a human being. If this were true, the departure of the soul would not be the end of life, and the soul would not be the center of perception. Since the soul must be the same as the life, theistic evolution cannot be the case.

In theistic evolution, creation is continuing. Man is still evolving. There is not a fixed nature that is possessed by all men. Since there would be a superior race, not all men are equal. Moral rights and responsibilities would not be equal. Morality itself would not be possible. Since this is incompatible with human rationality and divine justice, theistic evolution cannot be the case.

THE MORAL TELEOLOGICAL ARGUMENT:
Both Moral and Natural Evil Serve the Good

Natural evil in the form of toil and strife, and old age, sickness, and physical death, is not inherent in the creation, but must be due to moral evil. Moral evil is not due to free will, since it is possible to be free without the possibility of evil, as God is and man will be in the final state. Moral evil cannot be justified in terms of any virtue, since the virtues are themselves justified in relation to the good, and the virtues can be developed without moral evil. Moral evil can be justified only in relation to the good.

Morality assumes rationality, and man is fundamentally rational. Human desires and actions are determined by belief about what is good. The good for man as a rational being is the use of one's reason to the fullest. Since reason is used to understand the nature of things, good for man is knowledge. The greatest good is the highest knowledge, which is the knowledge of God. So, good for man is the knowledge of God. Evil for man is the denial of one's nature, that is, the failure to use or the denial of one's reason. Since God's existence and nature are clear to reason, evil is failure to know God or the denial of one's reason to avoid what is clear about God. The inherent consequence of the denial of one's reason is meaninglessness or spiritual death and all its natural effects in human nature.

Moral evil could be prevented by God, but is permitted by God in order to serve the divine purpose. Evil as unbelief serves subjectively to obscure and objectively to deepen the revelation of the divine justice and goodness. As creation reveals the divine nature, so redemption deepens that revelation. Through the experience of spiritual death, the revelation of God's justice is deepened. By restoration to life, to the knowledge of God, the revelation of God's goodness is deepened. This assumes knowledge of God is only through the creation.

If moral evil as unbelief is removed abruptly, the revelation is not deepened. If moral evil as unbelief is not removed, the revelation will not be seen. Evil as unbelief is allowed to work itself out in all its forms in the process of world history. Unbelief is removed gradually in world history. All nations will be brought to the knowledge of God. The earth will be filled with the knowledge of God as the waters cover the sea. Good overcomes evil.

The historical argument: on the existence and nature of redemption and its revelation. Human history must be understood in light of the existence of God, moral evil, and natural evil. Natural evil is not punishment for moral evil, but is imposed by God on man as a call to think deeply about the good. This call to repentance assumes forgiveness and the satisfaction of divine justice. The existence and nature of redemption requires special revelation. Special revelation must be consistent with what can be known of God from general revelation. Special revelation must be from God, given the nature of evil.

FOUNDATION IN GENERAL AND
SPECIAL REVELATION

Foundational beliefs for theism must be found in both general and special revelation. These beliefs include beliefs about the existence and nature of God, God's purpose in creation, the nature of man and human purpose, the nature of good and evil, the origin of evil, and the outcome of the conflict between good and evil in history.

Foundational beliefs for theism as found in Scripture (special revelation/SR) must be found from the very beginning. They should be found in the earliest chapters of Genesis and should be knowable from general revelation (GR) as well. The following is an outline summary of how this may be done.

God the Creator: His Existence and Nature

GR: By showing that there must be something eternal and that only some is eternal, it can be shown that God the Creator exists, that God is timeless, and that time began with the creation, that creation is *ex nihilo*, that creation *ex nihilo* shows God is all knowing and all powerful, that God is personal, sovereign, and infinitely good. The existence and nature of God are clearly revealed by the creation so that unbelief is without excuse. This is clear by reason so that faith is based upon reason and grows as understanding grows.

SR: In the beginning, God created the heavens and the earth: There is no time before the beginning. Time began with the creation. God is timeless in his eternality. Only God is eternal, all else is temporal, created *ex nihilo*. God, therefore, has total knowledge of and power over what he brought into being. God is personal, sovereign, and infinitely good. Scripture does not prove the existence of God, but assumes we can know this; it does not discuss God's nature, but assumes we have an understanding of the divine nature.

Creation Is Revelation

GR: Every being acts according to its nature and reveals its nature by its acts. Therefore, all things that exist and are ruled by God reveal the divine nature. There is no revelation of God apart from his work of creation and providence. There is no direct seeing of God.

SR: And God saw that it was good: God knows what is good and evil not by discovery, but by determination; there is no standard apart from himself. Good is what is pleasing to God according to his nature, according to his plan, his will, and purpose. The creation was what God wanted it to be. It revealed his nature, and this revelation was pleasing to him and, therefore, good. The heavens declare the glory of

God. The whole earth is full of his glory. He works all things after the counsel of his will to the praise of his glory.

Special Creation

GR: The diversity and order of the creation is by design and not by the present, natural processes. The act of bringing into being (creation) is other than the act of sustaining in being (providence). Differences are of kind and not merely of degree. Forms are not continuously changing; creation is completed. Evolution denies the difference between creation and providence, denies differences of kinds, denies the reality of essential forms, denies the original goodness of creation, denies the nature of human life, and denies the completion of creation.

SR: And God said, let there be . . . and it was so; and God created . . . each after its own kind. Evolution, whether of the heavens or the earth or the plants and the animals, by the present natural processes, cannot be harmonized with special creation of each form and kind by the Word of God. Evolution cannot be made consistent with the biblical account of the creation of human life, with the absence of natural evil in the original state of creation and in the completion of the creation. Creation is not the process of providence.

The Nature of Man

GR: All persons always have a formal aspect of their nature that constitutes their humanity regardless of changes in their moral condition. This aspect of their nature distinguishes them from all other kinds of beings, particularly animals. Man is distinguished from the animals by his capacity to understand. Man's nature is fundamentally rational. Within the nature of man, there is diversity and complexity in unity through the good. Good for man as a rational being is the use of his reason to the fullest. Reason is used to understand the nature of the creation and, thereby, the nature of the Creator. Hence, good for man is the knowledge of God. Evil is the denial of one's nature as a rational being and its consequences.

SR: Man is made in the image of God: he is finite, temporal, and changeable in his being, wisdom, power, holiness, justice, goodness, and truth. This is the larger or formal aspect of human nature possessed by all persons at all times.

Man is made from the dust of the ground, and God breathed into him the breath of life and he became a living creature. Man is, therefore, a body/soul unity. The soul is not infused into an already living being, but is the life of that being from its beginning. The body/soul unity implies the absence of physical death in the beginning and the necessity of the resurrection of the body with the removal of sin. The nature of the soul is spiritual, capable of surviving the death of the body.

Man is a male/female unity. What was originally one became two, and were to become one again. Male and female are complementary; they are a diversity held in unity by common commitment to the purpose of their creation—the achievement of the knowledge of God. Man is a triune personality, created in knowledge, holiness, and righteousness. This is the narrower aspect of human nature, the heart of man, which is changeable. It is the basis of man's function as prophet, priest, and king in the creation, the source of the diversity of man's gifts and calling. Unity and order in these functions are retained only where the good, eternal life, the knowledge of God is clearly understood and kept in mind.

Man is created for dominion over the creatures; he is given understanding by which he is to rule over the creation. He is to name the creation by developing all the powers latent in himself and in the creation. In naming the creation, he is to know the nature of the creation and, through this, know the nature of God the Creator. Dominion is for knowledge. Man has two ways placed before him, good and evil, represented symbolically in the two trees, the way of life and the way of death. The way of life is the pursuit of the good, the knowledge of God. The way of death is the pursuit of evil. It is the rejection of God's determination of the good as Creator for man's determination of the good apart from God.

Man is created in a corporate or covenantal unity. The Garden is the center from which all human life flows. In the first man is represented the corporate headship of the human race. Mankind will be confirmed in life or death by the decision of its corporate head.

The Original State of Creation

GR: Since God is all powerful and all good, he could and would make a world without any natural evil. Therefore, he must have and did so originally. Natural evil must be explained in terms of moral evil in a way that serves God's ultimate purpose in creating, that is, the revelation of his glory.

SR: And God saw everything that he had made, and behold, it was very good. There was no physical death of man in the original creation. Animals were given the vegetation for food; they did not devour each other. Toil and strife, and old age, sickness, and death are not inherent in the creation. They were imposed because of sin and will be removed as sin is removed.

Hope/The Sabbath

GR: Man's work is not an end in itself; it is a means to the end, the good, which is the knowledge of God. Work apart from the good is meaningless. To try to possess the good apart from work is vain hope. True work and true hope are inseparable. It must be certain that the good will be attained. Mankind, through its corporate, historical work, will attain the knowledge of God.

SR: And God blessed the seventh day and made it holy. God worked and completed his work. The sabbath commemorates this. Man is made in the image of God. He, too, must work and will complete his work. The sabbath affirms this hope. The work of dominion will be completed. The earth will be filled with the knowledge of God as the waters cover the sea.

Moral Evil and Sin and Death

GR: Good for man is what is in accordance with his nature; evil is what is contrary to his nature. Man is fundamentally rational. His desires and actions flow from his beliefs about what is good and real. Good for man as a rational being is the use of his reason to the fullest. Reason is used to understand the nature of the world and of the origin of the world (God). Hence, good for man is the knowledge of God.

Evil for man as a rational being is the failure to use one's reason, failure to understand. It is to be without the knowledge of God in unbelief. The inherent consequence of the denial of one's nature by the denial of reason is meaninglessness.

SR: The temptation in the Garden is not the cause of sin. It revealed that man had not been following the way of life, that he had not been seeking the knowledge of God. The failure to do what is right was rooted in not seeking God and in not retaining understanding of God's nature. Believing "you shall not surely die" implied that God was lying or ignorant and hence not God. Believing "you shall be like God knowing good and evil" implied that there is not a radical difference between the infinite Creator and the finite creature. One has to shut one's eyes, deny one's reason, to fail to see that human beings are finite. The inherent consequence of the denial of reason, the original sin, is spiritual death in the form of meaninglessness, boredom, and guilt.

Redemption

GR: The existence of human history with moral evil, spiritual death, and natural evil shows that full judgment has been withheld, that man is being called to repentance, to stop and think deeply about the cause of the human condition. The call to repentance assumes the promise of forgiveness. That man has forgiveness and how he is forgiven requires redemptive revelation. Scripture, as redemptive revelation, assumes the existence of sin in the denial of clear general revelation of the existence and nature of God. Scripture is the Word of God because it is spoken in the name of God (it is consistent with what is clearly revealed in general revelation about God), and what is spoken in the name of God can only be from God, given the nature of sin in all men, which denies general revelation.

SR: Man rejects God's first call to repentance (shame) through self-deception (the covering of leaves). He rejects the second call ("Where are you?") through self-justification. The third call to repentance comes with a promise ("the seed of the woman shall bruise the head of the serpent") and the curse (toil, strife, and physical death). Man repents and believes (he calls his wife's name Eve). He is covered (justified) through the death of another (the coats of skin). He is expelled from the Garden and must go through physical death. In sin, man must come to the knowledge of God through suffering. Sanctification is through suffering. There is no lasting life without the knowledge of God.

AN INTRODUCTION TO CHRISTIANITY

There are two teachings that define the foundation and goal of the Christian faith. The first (the foundation) is the teaching of the clarity of general revelation. This includes the nature and existence of God the Creator (Romans 1) and the law of God written on the hearts of all men (Romans 2). The second (the goal) is the teaching that eternal life is knowing God (John 17).

These two teachings on general revelation and eternal life are necessary for understanding every other teaching of Christianity, and without these two, no other teaching could make sense. Although these teachings are of central importance, they are almost altogether absent from popular Christianity and quite neglected in the historical understanding of Christianity. Their absence accounts for the direction of much of modern Christian thought since the Enlightenment and for the present weakened state of Christianity in its conflict with other visions of the world.

I would like to draw attention to these teachings in order that the task given to all mankind in Adam and now restored in Christ may be completed.

The clarity of general revelation is necessary to establish the existence and nature of sin and its inherent consequence of spiritual death. If there is no clear general revelation, there can be no sin, and if there is no sin, then the gospel message of forgiveness and redemption makes no sense. St. Paul said what may be known of God, his eternal power and divine nature have been clearly seen, being understood from the things that are made so that men are without excuse.[3] Here, clarity of revelation is what removes excuses and thereby establishes sin.

---

3. *Romans 1:19-20.*

It is incumbent, therefore, upon those who would bring the message of God's forgiveness to show not only that God exists, but that it is clear that God exists and that the sin of which man must repent consists precisely of failing to see and believe this clear revelation.

The common belief that man is seeking God implies the denial of the clarity of general revelation and of sin and is flatly rejected by the apostles and the prophets: none seek God, no, not one (Romans 3). If there is no moral evil (unbelief in the face of clear revelation), the existence of natural evil (physical death) is inexplicable, and the work of Christ as savior is pointless.

The clarity of general revelation is particularly directed to the eternality of God, that God is eternal and nothing besides God is eternal. This is the affirmation of Genesis 1: In the beginning, God created the heavens and the earth. This clarity is such that no education is necessary to see it, and it can overcome any level of sophisticated objection. It is clear through and through. As St. Paul says, any argument against the knowledge of God is to be demolished.[4] The clarity is such that any seeking to know God will know God. But more than that. The clarity so presses in on man that one has to stop thinking (close one's eyes/understanding) to avoid seeing it and even harden oneself in one's suffering to avoid thinking about the root cause of suffering.

How is it known then that only God is eternal, that the natural world is not eternal, nor is the soul of man eternal? What does it mean to say that the moral law is known to all? And what does it mean to say eternal life is knowing God? These things are known through natural theology and the moral law.

---

4. *2 Corinthians 10:4-5.*

———

PART III

ETHICS

———

Chapter 4

——

THE MORAL LAW

THE CONCEPT OF THE GOOD

THE CONCEPT OF THE GOOD IS NOT an arbitrary concept. It is grounded in the reality of choice. Choice assumes values, and values assume the concept of the good. Ethics is concerned with giving a rational justification for the answer to the question "what is the good?" In making choices, some things are chosen as means to ends, and some things are chosen as ends in themselves and not for the sake of anything else. The good is what is chosen as an end in itself. Choice is made when there are competing desires, both of which cannot be fulfilled. The internal conflict is resolved by considering which alternative best serves the good. The good, therefore, is that which is of the highest value and the source of unity, the final arbiter in moral conflicts.

The good is not to be confused with the means to the good or with the effect of possessing the good. Virtue is the means to the good, and happiness is the effect of possessing what we believe is the good. The good is neither virtue nor happiness. The good is the moral absolute. The moral concepts of virtue and happiness are to be understood in relation to the good; the good is not to be understood in relation to them. In this sense, ethics is teleological; it is oriented to the goal of the good. It is not oriented to the consequence of possessing the good, which is sometimes taken as the good. Nor is it oriented to virtue or what is right or duty, which is sometimes taken as the good. Ethics focused on duty or on happiness fails to see the distinctiveness of the good and are misdirected from the start.

Ethics focused on duty is called deontological ethics. It sets itself in contrast to and in conflict with ethics focused on happiness, which is utilitarian ethics. Kant and Mill represent deontology and utilitarian ethics, respectively. Most contemporary ethics is either deontological or utilitarian. The dispute between them remains unresolved because of uncritically held assumptions about the good. They are antinomies, polar opposites, both of which are mistaken because of a common faulty view about the good.

Deontology takes the achievement of the good as a consequence of doing what is right and treats the good as a form of consequentialism, in the same category as utilitarianism. It puts the good and happiness in the same category and treats consequentialism as somewhat submoral. It is not morally fitting to be motivated by consequences. When motivated by consideration of consequences, duty loses its moral worth, according to deontologists. Duty is to be done for its own sake, not for an extrinsic reward. It is true that the good is a consequence of virtue; virtue, after all, is the means to the good. But it is the inherent consequence of virtue when virtue is properly understood, that is, understood in light of the good. And happiness is the inherent consequence of the good, and only indirectly is happiness the consequence of virtue. Further, the happiness accompanying the possession of the good is not to be identified with the pleasures accompanying the satisfaction of a sensual appetite. There are qualitative differences between the pleasures of knowledge and the pleasures of food. Mill rightly protested, that it is better to be a Socrates dissatisfied than a pig satisfied, even though he could not justify his protest due to his identifying pleasure with the good.

In addition to this, deontologists must separate virtue and duty from its natural consequence of the good and thereby introduce an inherent arbitrariness into the duty of the moral law, which, in teleology, is the means to the good. Problems arise when attempts are made to overcome this arbitrariness by appeal to reason alone as lawgiver, independent of a consideration of human nature and what determines that nature. Nor is the arbitrariness overcome by the universalizing of reason apart from the good, which gives limit and unity to the moral law. A further problem of arbitrariness remains in reconnecting virtue and happiness in the absence of the good.

Utilitarian consequentialists rightly see that duty is not to be pursued for its own sake, but for the sake of the good. But identifying the good with happiness or with pleasure introduces several problems to which deontologists and others properly object. Whether pleasure can be pursued for its own sake, whether it can overcome the antinomy of egoism and altruism, whether it allows for injustice, whether it preserves human dignity, and whether it can distinguish moral and non-moral motivations are continuing problems for utilitarianism.

All of this is to say that if the good as the basic concept of ethics is not clearly distinguished from virtue as its means and happiness as its effect, we soon become involved in unending disputes, which then are taken as justification for skepticism. However, a little attention helps us to see these need not be confused.

Virtue is not the good, whether the virtue is instrumental, natural, or moral. Money is an instrumental virtue. Money is not sought for its own sake, but as a means to something else, for things it can buy. House and food likewise are sought for their instrumental value. Natural virtues which we have by natural endowment, such as health and talent, are not ends in themselves, but help us in achieving the good. Staying alive is not the good, but we stay alive to seek the good. Courage and wisdom are not the good, but are moral virtues that enable us to achieve the good. Love is not the good, but in loving someone, we seek the good for them. The loved one is not the good, but one for whom the good is sought.

Happiness is not the good, nor are variations of happiness, such as peace, comfort, and pleasure. Happiness is the effect of possessing what we believe is the good. Happiness changes as belief about the good changes. Both what is possessed and the belief about its being good are necessary for happiness.

THE MORAL LAW

Some things about morality are clear. Skeptics deny this. It is what is basic about morality that is clear. The good is the most basic moral concept. The moral law is the means to the good. Since the good for human beings and the moral law are based on human nature, and some things about human nature are clear, some things about morality are clear. In what follows, I will try to show how the moral law is clear because it is grounded in basic things about human nature that are clear.

What are some things that are clear about human nature? We make choices of means and ends; we think of the less basic in light of the more basic; we are one being and seek unity in our being; we work and hope for results; we are born ignorant and need teaching; we live in a human society; we are born of the union of male and female; we value some things more than others; we seek to be treated fairly; we long for what we believe is the good. From these simple and clear aspects of human nature, there arise moral laws with implications that apply to all dimensions of life.

How can we go from these simple observations to moral laws, not to mention laws having implications for all dimensions of life? Here I will make a summary sketch of each moral law.[1]

Moral Law 1: The Good and God

There is a moral absolute in each person. It is their source of unity. One's moral absolute must be justified by one's view of human nature, which is justified by one's view of what is real. Justification by what is real is opposed to relativism. What is real, whether all or only some is eternal, is clear. Clear means one can know if one seeks to know or one has to stop thinking to avoid seeing what is clear.

It is clear that only some is eternal: that matter is not eternal (self-maintaining) and that the soul is not eternal (it grows in knowledge). What is eternal brings into being or creates what is not eternal. Thus, the Creator of the nature of beings is the determiner of what is good for each being. Creation or theism is opposed to pantheism, polytheism, atheism, materialism, dualism, and shamanism. Clarity is opposed to skepticism and fideism (knowledge is not possible), to mysticism (feeling is independent of thought), and to voluntarism (will is independent of intellect).

The origin of moral evil is the failure to use one's reason or the denial of one's reason. The consequences inherent in moral evil are meaninglessness, boredom, and guilt. Understanding what is the good is the source of unity between all persons in all of life.

---

1. For a more comprehensive exposition of the Moral Law, see: Gangadean, *Philosophical Foundation*, Chapters 9-19.

Moral Law 2: Thinking and Presupposition

Thinking is presuppositional. We must think of the less basic in light of the more basic. Meaning is logically prior to truth; basic belief is logically prior to the meaning of experience; concepts are logically ordered (the infinite and eternal are logically prior to the finite and temporal), and premises are logically prior to the conclusion. We must think of the finite in light of the infinite (man in light of God); not the infinite in light of the finite (God in light of man) or the finite in light of the finite (man in light of nature).

Rational Presuppositionalism is opposed to empiricism (all knowledge is from sense experience) and to rationalism (reason is first a source of truth rather than a test for meaning).

When there are persisting disputes, it is necessary to examine uncritically held assumptions for meaning. Disputes between and within each form of theism (Judaism, Christianity, Islam, and Deism) are all rooted in misconceptions regarding the infinite attributes of deity. Infinite is mistakenly thought of in light of the finite. The cumulative effects of misconceiving God's nature are divisions and cultural collapse.

Moral Law 3: Integrity and Knowledge

Integrity is necessary and sufficient for knowledge. Integrity is a concern for logical consistency within our beliefs and between our professed beliefs and our actions. It is the source of unity within a person. Our most basic and implicit profession is a concern to know. Our most explicit profession is expressed by an oath or vow.

Self-examination is necessary for integrity. We can know if we believe what we profess by looking at our actions. We can know if our ideas are logically consistent by reflection and by dialogue. If a belief is unlivable, we cannot, with integrity, profess that belief.

Discipline is necessary for integrity. Discipline requires diligence in the use of ordinary means to attain one's goal. A lack of discipline implies a lack of concern. A lack of knowledge about what is clear implies a lack of integrity. Lack of integrity is immediately experienced as guilt.

Integrity is opposed to hypocrisy, which involves self-deception and self-justification. Integrity is opposed to placing practical and psychological needs above concern for truth. The effects of continuing hypocrisy are increasing mental blindness and mindlessness.

Moral Law 4: Work and Hope

The goal of all work is the good. Work is not an end in itself. Work is necessary to achieve the good. The good is knowledge of the nature of things (logos) and of the origin of their nature (God). Knowledge as the good is unending, inexhaustible, comprehensive, inalienable, cumulative, communal, fulfilling, corporate, ultimate, and transformative.

The fullness of knowledge can only be attained through the work of dominion, which is corporate and historical. By dominion, the powers latent in the creation are developed fully. The goal of work is to attain the fullness of knowledge. The earth is to be filled with the knowledge of God. It is certain that the goal will be attained.

This view is opposed to no hope (the good cannot be attained by work) and to false hope (that the good can be attained apart from work). Both views distort the nature of work and the good. Work apart from the good becomes meaningless.

Moral Law 5: Authority and Insight

Authority is based on insight into the good and the means to it. It is not based on might. It is rational, not personal. It is historically cumulative, not individual. Authority based on insight must be honored; authority without insight must be changed where possible.

There is an order in all our functions. In each person, the order is intellect, emotions, and will. In each institution, the same order of our functions must be observed. The philosophical function must lead the psychological and the practical.

Among institutions, no institution is total; each is equally under the moral law according to its form and function. Neither family, state, Church, nor business may subordinate any other institution to its own end. Historically, each has distorted the others for a time. Authority is opposed to the state over Church and Church over the state; to state over family and family over the state; to business over the state and state over business. Authority is opposed to subordinating family to the state in public education on the assumption that education is neutral with respect to assuming a world and life view.

Moral Law 6: Human Dignity and Rationality

Human dignity is rooted in the capacity to understand. Human society is a society of rational beings who can reason with each other. Freedom in this society is determined by the exercise of one's capacity to understand. To hold each other responsible for the use of reason is to affirm human dignity. To dehumanize is to deny this capacity in oneself or in another person. To deny this capacity in another, one must first have denied it in oneself.

Human dignity is opposed to the use of force (murder or war) to change the behavior of others. It seeks to deal with the most basic beliefs that shape feelings and behavior. Human dignity is opposed to all forms of racism or multiculturalism, which deny the common human essence in the capacity to understand. Human dignity is opposed to all gender conflicts, which arise from a failure to find unity in diversity in achieving the good through the use of reason to the fullest.

Human dignity is opposed to the denial of the capacity to understand from conception. Human dignity is opposed to not holding a person accountable for the failure to use reason which leads to behavior destructive to human society.

Human dignity is opposed to intervention to preserve human life where the capacity to understand has been irretrievably lost. Human dignity is opposed to forms of discipline which hinder one's capacity to understand or which denies that natural evil is a call to think deeply about basic issues.

Moral Law 7: Friendship and Marriage

Friendship is the effect of mutual commitment to the good. Friends are those who share the deepest concerns. True friendship is lasting. Friendship is not the good itself as in romantic love, nor a means to an end as in a utilitarian relationship. It is not love, which is to be directed to all, nor natural affection, which is directed to the familiar.

Mutual commitment to the good is both necessary and sufficient for friendship. No other qualification can make friendship possible nor hinder its occurrence. Marriage as a lifelong relationship that shares the deepest concerns must be based on friendship.

Marriage is constituted by a physical union, which is by nature mutual and simultaneous, the outward sign of giving oneself to the other to become one. The natural relation between the sign and the reality determines the natural limits of human sexuality.

Moral Law 8: Value and Talent

No one values all things equally. Value is a function of supply and demand. Demand is a function of belief about the good. Supply is a function of the use of talent. Talent is an aspect of our being. It is an ability to achieve some aspect of the good. No one has all talent. Everyone has some talent.

The source of talent is not from others or of ourselves, but from the source of our being. Talent is given to each for all. We contribute to others by the creativity of our talent, and we receive from others by their creativity. Talent is realized as the uniqueness of one's personality. Vision of the good activates talent; talent, when developed, forms its function.

Talent is developed in the service and achievement of others and by personal discipline. Lasting value is a function of the use of talent in pursuit of the good. Man is neither individually nor collectively the origin of talent, so man can neither individually nor collectively be the absolute owner of what has value. Man is not owner, but steward, in contrast to capitalism and socialism. Regard for the good determines regard for talent. Wages and prices are truly valued only in relation to the good. The essence of stealing is the failure to develop one's talent in pursuit of the good in service to others.

Moral Law 9: Truth and Justice

Truth is necessary and sufficient for justice. Justice is first distributive, then contractual, and then retributive. Speaking the whole truth is necessary to prevent and correct injustice. Speaking the whole truth is an activity of all of one's life. To prevent injustice, one must know what is just and the root causes of injustice.

To speak the truth, one must seek to know the truth and to communicate the truth. Ignorance and sincerity do not excuse failure to speak the truth. Decisions affecting others are not private. They are subject to public examination. Since speech is rational, freedom of speech is a right to rational discourse. Not to speak the truth is to share in injustice and its consequence.

Moral Law 10: Suffering and The Good

Discontent arises from a failure to understand the good and the means to the good. It is the source of envy and all inordinate desire. No virtue, moral, natural, or instrumental is the good, but the means to the good. Neither happiness nor pleasure is the good, but is the effect of possessing what is believed to be the good. Suffering arises when we believe we cannot have the good.

Suffering is not self-certifying; one can be insensible to one's suffering. The significance of physical death and its causes depends on one's basic beliefs. All natural evil is due to moral evil—the failure to use one's reason. In theism, no natural evil is necessary. If God is all good and all powerful, then toil and strife, and old age, sickness, and physical death are not originally necessary. Just consequences are necessary and inherent, not imposed. Since natural evil is not an inherent consequence of moral evil, it is not punishment. The inherent consequence of moral evil is spiritual, not physical death.

Suffering, when understood, serves the good. When misunderstood, it is avoided as useless or as a hindrance to the good. Natural evil is imposed to restrain, to recall from, and to remove moral evil and its inherent consequences. All things are seen to work together for good to those who seek the good.

PART IV

HISTORY OF PHILOSOPHY:
SUMMARY AND CRITIQUE

Chapter 5

———

ON PHILOSOPHY

WHAT IS PHILOSOPHY?

P HILOSOPHY MAY BE DEFINED IN TERMS of its several features: it is an area, an attitude, a method, an application, and a system.

Philosophy Is an Area: The Foundation and Goal

Philosophy deals with the most basic questions we can think about in each of its three branches. The most fundamental area of philosophy is epistemology. Epistemology asks the question: How do I know? The basic questions of epistemology include: Is knowledge of basic things (concerning the existence and nature of God and man and of good and evil) possible? Is knowledge of basic things necessary, or is belief based on testimony (human or divine) sufficient? How is knowledge of basic things possible? Is it by sense experience (in science) or by intuition (in art, morality, or religion), or by reason (in philosophy)?

The next field of philosophy is metaphysics. Metaphysics addresses the question: What ultimately exists? Ontology is the aspect of metaphysics that addresses whether everything is matter, or does spirit also exist, or whether everything is all spirit only. Cosmology asks is everything eternal in some form or other or is only some (God) eternal, or is nothing eternal? These are the basic questions of metaphysics.

The last major field of philosophy is ethics. Ethics deals with the question: What ought I to do? Basic ethical questions to consider include: Is there an end in itself, something to be sought for its own sake, a highest good, a goal of life? Is this good the same for all? Can it be known? Is morality possible if basic things are not objectively clear (knowable by all who seek to know)?

Because philosophy deals with the basic questions based on general revelation (what is knowable to all), philosophy is basic to all other disciplines. Philosophy is basic to the sciences, to the arts, and to religions that are based on special revelation. These questions of philosophy are the most basic of all questions. No other discipline besides philosophy attempts to answer these. Answers to the basic questions must be known and cannot be assumed. Lastly, philosophy is necessary as the foundation of all other disciplines.

Philosophy Is an Attitude: The Love of Wisdom

The term "philosophy" literally means love of wisdom. One has wisdom if one knows the good and the means to the good. Beliefs about what is real and what is the good affect our desires and choices, and so are crucially important. Failure to know and to seek the good is the source of all the miseries of life. Fear of not having the good is the beginning of wisdom. Love of the good brings one to the fullness of wisdom.

Wisdom is possible and necessary for all and not only for some people. In the Wisdom literature, the Simple disregards the need for wisdom, and the Fool thinks he already possesses wisdom. One cannot seek wisdom if one is mistaken about being wise. Furthermore, philosophy cannot be pursued without the love of wisdom.

Philosophy Is a Method: The Critical Use of Reason

By reason is meant the laws of thought. By way of reminder, these are the law of identity—*a* is *a*; the law of non-contradiction—not both *a* and *non-a*, at the same time and in the same respect; and the law of excluded middle—either *a* or *non-a*. Reason is the test for meaning. Reason is used critically when basic beliefs are tested for meaning. The meaning of a statement is more basic than the truth of a statement: one has to know its meaning before knowing its truth. A statement lacks meaning if it violates a law of thought. A statement which lacks meaning cannot be true.

It is necessary to test basic beliefs for meaning. Reason is the test for meaning. There can be no truth without meaning. We ought to use reason critically to test basic beliefs for meaning.

Philosophy Is an Application: Self-Examination

The first application of philosophy is to identify one's own basic beliefs and test them for meaning. Self-examination is necessary for integrity and integrity is necessary and sufficient for knowledge. "The unexamined life is not worth living" is attributed to Socrates, who is highly regarded among philosophers. To live an unconscious and uncritical life is less than the life of reason and is, therefore, less than human existence. Unthinking life for humans is wasted life.

We can fail to identify basic beliefs. We can falsely identify our own basic beliefs. We can use reason to criticize other beliefs, but fail to think critically about our own basic beliefs through self-examination. If we lack knowledge of basic things, this is an indicator that we lack integrity.

Philosophy Is a System: World and Life View

Philosophy uses reason to construct a coherent world and life view on the foundation of basic beliefs. A worldview supplies meaning to all of life. A worldview is applied to life by shaping attitudes and values which come to expression in the institutions of cultures and civilizations. Worldviews are held more or less consciously and more or less consistently in every culture and civilization. There are internal and external challenges of reason to the consistency of every worldview. Many cultures and civilizations have ceased to exist when their worldview ceased to be credible.

Philosophy is fundamentally relevant to all of life. Thinking by nature is presuppositional. If there is agreement on what is more basic, there will be agreement on what is less basic. All worldviews are not equally coherent. A culture or civilization will not survive if its worldview fails to achieve coherence when challenged.

FOUNDATION FOR PHILOSOPHY OF HISTORY[1]

Rational Presuppositionalism advocates for the above approach to philosophy. Some may want to spend years pouring through every

---

1. This section was drafted by The Logos Foundation Editorial Board. The ideas were taken from a lecture delivered by Dr. Gangadean on the history of philosophy at Logos Theological Seminary, 2008.

page of Plato, to master all the nuances and keep up to date on what each new scholar says, but that is not our concern. With Plato and with every other philosopher, we are going to bring *that* to *this*. The clarity of general revelation provides the objective grounds by which to assess the consistency and coherence of the philosophers studied. One should not just forget that some things are clear when one reads Plato. When one looks at Aristotle, one should want to know if he was able to overcome the shortcomings of Socrates, Plato, and the Presocratics; did he see what is clear, or did he get trapped in antinomies because he was trapped in a dualistic framework? Did uncritically held assumptions lead to insufficient responses to the perennial questions of philosophy?

If someone wants to object by saying: "you're not really doing the history of philosophy, you are just presenting your own ideas," the response is twofold. First, it is not who is to say, but what is to say. One should not be interested in who answered what, but in what was answered, and whether or not those answers are sound. Is the answer attained sufficient to set us free from ignorance and unbelief? If some things are clear, if the basic things are clear, then one should be able to identify why the philosophers throughout history have not been able to find knowledge and reach unity, and then one can press on and make progress rather than operating under problematic philosophical assumptions that fail to settle unresolved disputes. Going through the history of philosophy just to chronicle nuances within and among philosophers is tantamount to wasted effort, since the basic questions remain unanswered. Philosophy is not philosophy if it forsakes the big questions that only philosophy can answer. These are the questions of epistemology (how is knowledge possible?), metaphysics (what is real/eternal?), and ethics (what ought I to do?).

The second response, though, is that we are following the model established by Socrates. The Sophists did not do philosophy: they practiced the art of persuasion rather than engaging with the basic questions. They talked *about* philosophy, but did not *do* philosophy. When people try to do philosophy, pressure comes from others to discontinue. One may think, "not today; now we are enlightened." Remember, it was a democracy that voted to execute Socrates: people do not want to undergo critique. Humans do not want to examine their lives or have their tradition questioned. Socrates was accused of corrupting the youth and teaching other gods than what the city believed in, which is against popular religion, and the masses did not want to hear that. So, they silenced Socrates through execution in order to avoid confronting the gadfly that called them to think about basic things.

Many engage in the history of philosophy and never engage with the basic questions. Rational Presuppositionalism approaches the basic questions from the most basic (epistemology) to the less basic (metaphysics and ethics). One is to understand the latter in light of the former. The pattern of challenge and response will be traced in each thinker and philosophical school of thought. First, one should identify the challenges that philosophers encountered in the past, see to what extent they were able to overcome them, and try to understand what uncritically held assumptions held them back when they did not overcome. That is in keeping with Socrates' call to live the examined life.

One should want to examine the philosophers of the past and their teaching to critically analyze their ideas in light of what is clear. That is what is meant by saying that one is to bring *that* to *this* rather than *this* to *that*. One should not get bogged down in the details. People labour much pouring over texts to try to find a coherent position, to try to find the truth in one philosopher or another, but often it is hard to find coherence because, in many cases, a consistent position was not arrived at. That type of pursuit is not consistent with the spirit of philosophy as the love of wisdom. In wisdom, one seeks to know the good and the means to it. The good is grounded in the real, and the real is known by the critical use of reason—by testing ideas for coherence and meaning. Philosophy is the discipline that deals with basic questions. And what is our knowledge about if not about basic things, about what is eternal (God *or* not) and about human nature (man), and about what we ought to do as human beings (about good and evil)? If philosophy is not about what is clear to reason about God and man and good and evil, what is it about?

The five components below are operating assumptions in thinking about the philosophy of history and, by implication, the history of philosophy. They together constitute a foundation for engaging with the history of philosophy.[2]

Meaning and Worldview

Human beings, as thinking beings, seek to make sense of their world by forming a worldview. Presuppositions are the basic beliefs we use to interpret our experience. No experience is meaningful without interpretation. Experiences are interpreted differently in varying worldviews. A worldview must be internally coherent in order to retain meaning.

Basic Beliefs

There are two alternative basic beliefs in each foundational feature of a worldview: in epistemology, in metaphysics, and in ethics. These basic beliefs are contradictories, not contraries; both cannot be true, and both cannot be false; one must be true and the other false.

In epistemology: either knowledge is possible, or knowledge is not possible. If knowledge is possible, then in principle: some things are clear; the basic things are clear; the basic things (about God and man and good and evil) are clear to reason. If knowledge of basic things is not possible, then either skepticism or fideism results, both of which lead to nihilism (the loss of all meaning).

In metaphysics: either all is eternal in some form or other, or only some is eternal. If all is eternal, then either matter or spirit or both or neither (i.e., nothing) is eternal. If only some is eternal, then what is eternal brought into existence (created) what is not eternal.

In ethics: either there is rational justification for the good (the moral absolute), or there is no such justification. The good is grounded in human nature, which is determined by what is eternal. If what is eternal cannot be known, then human nature cannot be known, and there can be no rational justification for the good.

---

2. Surrendra Gangadean, *Foundation for Philosophy of History* (Phoenix: Logos Papers Press, 2014), Logos Paper No. 19. See: https://thelogospapers.com

Consciousness and Consistency

Human beings are more or less conscious and consistent in holding their basic beliefs. There is an admixture of contradictory beliefs in each person. One of the contradictory beliefs is existentially more basic and, therefore, more prevailing in each person. One's consciousness and consistency depend on one's presupposition, personality, background, and mood. We should seek to be more conscious and consistent.

History and Conflict

History is the outworking of these conflicting beliefs in each person, in each culture, and in world history. Suffering of toil and strife, and old age, sickness, and death (and collectively, of war, famine, and plague) challenges each person to make greater sense of the world. The conflict is between understanding and misunderstanding, between belief and unbelief. The conflict is between the use of reason (to act according to one's nature) and lack of the use of reason (to neglect, avoid, resist, or deny reason regarding what is clear). The conflict is between meaningfulness and meaninglessness, between life and death, between good and evil.

Reason and Hope

In the conflict between contradictory beliefs, only what is meaningful will last. Every form and degree of admixture between belief and unbelief will come to expression in culture in world history. The darkness of misunderstanding cannot overcome or withstand the demands of the light of reason in human nature. Evil serves only to deepen the revelation of the nature of things. In the spiritual war, which is age-long and agonizing, good will overcome evil.

Chapter 6

___

PRESOCRATIC PHILOSOPHY

T HE ATTEMPT TO EXPLAIN THE WORLD in terms of finite Greek
gods (Zeus, Apollo, etc.) was intellectually inadequate. The gods
were not eternal; their origin needed to be explained in terms of what
was eternal. Furthermore, the gods were somewhat arbitrary, in the
image of humans, with all the human failings. Symbolic interpretations of these stories that were initially psychologically or aesthetically
satisfying were not a substitute for rational explanation. Given man's
rational nature and ultimate need for meaning, a new beginning was
sought by the philosophically minded.

Thales of Miletus, a Greek thinker, living on the coast of Asia Minor
(c. 624–546 B.C.), began by rejecting personal for impersonal explanation and supernatural explanation for natural explanation. He said
all was made of one underlying material substance, and that substance
was water. This begins the material monist view in the western world,
a view which is implicitly or explicitly assumed in most of science
today. The project then is to show how the many aspects of the world
of human experience can be explained in terms of this one reality.
This is the problem of the one and the many, of unity and diversity, of
permanence and change, of appearance and reality.

Anaximander (c. 610–546 B.C.), also of Miletus, proposed an alternative answer. He said that all was made of an indeterminate stuff, the
Apeiron, which is boundless, having no particular quality. He probably reasoned that one could never explain how *non-a* (dryness) comes
from *a* (wetness, the essence of Thales' substance, water). The only
logical solution (assuming material monism) was to have an original
substance without any qualities, hence the *Apeiron*, perhaps like ener-

gy, only without any qualities. Still, this was a material substance, not spirit. He tries to explain everything in natural terms.

Anaximenes (c. 586–526 B.C.) did not accept this solution. He said instead that the original substance was air. If the *Apeiron* was truly without any quality, then it could not be distinguished from non-being, and being cannot arise from non-being. Perhaps air was a natural alternative since it was the closest thing to the indefinite and yet be distinguishable from non-being. However, air cannot explain non-air (wetness or earth or fire). It would appear material monism is at a dead end unless one of its premises can be changed: either deny permanence or change or that there is only one substance. This is what happens next.

Xenophanes (c. 570–478 B.C.) fled the Persian conquest of Ionia to Italy and Sicily. He was a critic of popular religion (gods made in the image of men) and proposed a pantheistic concept instead. This divine being is a unity containing all the diversity. In place of Milesian hylozoism (that matter is alive and is self-moving), he believed that the divine being was the source of change, although itself not undergoing change. But since God for Xenophanes is not transcendent (over and above nature), the change in nature would also be a change in God.

Pythagoras (c. 570–495 B.C.) introduced the belief in reincarnation and sought release for the soul through contemplation of the eternal. What was permanent was the essence of things, and that essence is numerical. Things are numbers, and numbers are things. Yet how essences come to form things that come to be and pass away is not explained.

Heraclitus (c. 535–475 B.C.) eliminated the problem of how the one permanent being can change to become the many things of human experience by denying the existence of any permanent reality. Everything is in a state of change. There is no permanent stuff underlying the change. Everything is fire, constantly in flux. There is a law, however that governs the process of change, and only this law is permanent. This law called *Logos* is the universal reason that pervades everything. Everything comes to pass according to this reason. But if change is according to reason, then *a* cannot come from *non-a*, nor can *a* come from non-being. The problem of being that is permanent remains.

Parmenides (c. 515–460 B.C.) of Elea in southern Italy developed the opposing position that permanence only is real, and change is only apparent; change does not really exist. Only what can be thought by reason is real; the senses do not give knowledge. This permanent reality is one, indivisible, unmoving, and immutable. Non-being cannot be thought and cannot exist; there is no empty space. His disciple Zeno tried to show through several paradoxes that motion as change in space and time is inexplicable and, therefore, unreal. To resolve the antinomies between Heraclitus and Parmenides, between senses and reason, between permanence and change, a new solution was sought in pluralism.

Empedocles (494–434 B.C.) in Sicily said there were four ultimate substances: earth, air, fire, and water. These were moved by two forces, love and hate. All of reality is to be explained in terms of the mixture of these four elements. In addition, the soul exists as distinct from the four material substances, surviving the body at death. But there are many more than four qualities. Can qualitative change be explained in terms of four elements without one quality becoming another quality and thus violating the principle of identity and permanence? Furthermore, love and hate and soul are not derivable from the four elements. These are personal and immaterial in nature.

Anaxagoras (500–428 B.C.) brought Milesian philosophy to Athens. He solved the problem of change by denying the one and affirming an infinite number of qualitatively different substances. All change results from admixture of various proportions of these different qualities. The source of change is by the activity of *Nous* or Mind or Reason, an immaterial and intelligent force that acts purposefully in the world. But if the many are ultimate, then there is no underlying unity, nothing common among the many by which they could be understood. And since all perceived qualities were admixtures and not a simple ultimate, what is real is unknowable, and what appears is not real. Also, since individual beings were admixtures, not real forms, *Nous* was merely a source of motion, not purpose. The world remained unintelligible.

Democritus (460–370 B.C.) of Abdera in northern Greece continued the Ionian philosophy of Leucippus, who formulated the atomic view as an outcome of earlier speculation. There are countless eternal, indivisible, unchanging units of being that are qualitatively identical. The qualities that are seen by the senses are not in these atoms, but relative to the perceiver. The atoms are not perceivable, but can be known only by reason. Atoms move in space, which is real. All reality is to be explained in terms of atoms and their movements and combinations. But if senses give appearances only, differences cannot be justified by reason either. For how can adding two identical units give any more than two of the same kind? Quality is distinct from quantity. The basic issues remain unresolved on the basis of material monism. This gave rise to the relativism and skepticism of the Sophists. Attention shifted from nature to man. Socrates took up the challenge of the Sophists.

The Sophists, like humanistic teachers today, brought learning, culture, and philosophy to the populace. Given the doubt concerning popular religion produced by the philosophers, who themselves were unable to answer the ultimate questions satisfactorily, this new breed of teachers based their teaching on skepticism and relativism. They taught pragmatism—how to achieve success—particularly through the use of rhetoric, the art of persuasion.

Protagoras (490–420 B.C.), one of the leading Sophists, taught that man (collectively) is the measure of all things. Since sense perception cannot give certainty, one person's judgment was as good as another's. All men are equal in this sense, and democracy is the natural form of government. Social codes are obeyed for selfish reasons. Education is the means of self-improvement.

Gorgias (483–375 B.C.) took skepticism to its logical conclusion. Both the senses and reason are futile. Nothing exists. If anything did exist, we could not know it. Even if we could know it, we could not communicate it. Deception is justifiable since all persuasion is rhetoric. He believed in an individualistic doctrine that might makes right, that culture is a psychological instrument of control. Politics is power, strictly.

Socrates (470–399 B.C.) of Athens saw the pretension and danger of the way of the Sophists. The oracle at Delphi said no one was wiser than Socrates. He saw the irony of this in the ignorance of the poets, politicians, and scientists who professed to know. He was a gadfly to his fellow Athenians in saying to them that the unexamined life was not worth living. He was a philosophical midwife to others, helping them through dialogue to bring forth and examine their ideas of justice, piety, pleasure, the good, and knowledge. He believed there were objective standards of morality that were knowable through the persistent critical use of reason. He was tried on the charge of corrupting the youth of Athens and for not believing in the gods that the city believes in. He chose death over giving up philosophizing. His life inspired many in his day and since to pursue philosophy.

Chapter 7

———

PLATO

HISTORICAL CONTEXT:
Skepticism and the Breakdown of
Traditional Greek Culture

PLATO (429–347 B.C.) WITNESSED THE COLLECTIVE failure of Greek culture. The supernatural explanations of the polytheistic worldview of Homer and Hesiod failed to provide a rational account of the nature of reality. The finite, human, all-too-human gods did not answer the perennial questions, but compounded the problem through anthropomorphic gods. The failure of polytheism was followed by the failure of naturalism. The Presocratic philosophers could not solve the problems of change and permanence, unity and diversity, appearance and reality. Their enterprise ended with the failure of nerve in the rise of skepticism (intellectual despair rooted in unexamined assumptions about what is infinite and eternal), which led to the cultural relativism and hedonism of the Sophists. Plato also witnessed the failure of Greek unity through the civil war between Athens and Sparta—democracy vs. aristocracy. Lastly, the failure of democracy affected Plato most acutely since Socrates, his teacher, was executed for exposing the ignorance of leaders without knowledge. The problem facing Plato was to show how knowledge is possible and to assure that those who have this knowledge will rule—the philosopher king. "Unless philosophers rule or those who rule philosophize [think deeply about basic things], there will be no end of trouble."[1]

---

1. Plato, *The Republic*, 473d-e.

PHILOSOPHICAL CONTEXT:
Epistemology and Metaphysics

Plato uncritically assumed that matter and the souls were eternal, as well as the forms and the Demiurge. He used reason constructively to develop a worldview based on these four eternal realities. The forms are the unchanging essences of things existing apart from things in themselves. These only can be the object of true knowledge, known by reason and not by the senses. The highest form, the form of all forms, is the form of the good. Matter is the substance out of which physical things are made; these things are copies of the forms, but since matter has its own identity, things are imperfect copies of the forms. The Divine Maker or Demiurge is not an absolute creator, but one who shapes matter into forms as far as matter and his power permits. Soul is the true self of a person at present existing in a body. The soul has knowledge of the forms prior to coming into this body. The senses obscure this prior knowledge. By recollection through reasoning one can come to a clear vision of the forms. These beliefs of Plato set the limit within which he answered the questions of ethics. To correct his ethics, he would have to examine his assumptions about the nature of reality.[2] In Plato's view, matter and the souls are both eternal and independent of each other. Plato offered no reason for believing the soul is eternal. And he did not consider any reasons against it. In this, he is not unlike many who hold basic beliefs without proof.

ETHICAL DUALISM:
A Person Is a Duality of Body and Soul

For Plato, evil is due to having a body. The senses and desires of the body hinder the soul, which is entirely good. The person consists of three parts: the intellect, will, and desires (appetites). Virtue consists of each part functioning properly. The corresponding virtues are wisdom, courage, and temperance. Justice, the fourth virtue, is the proper relation of the three parts. When the intellect rules the will and

---

2. For a critical analysis of Plato's metaphysical assumptions, see Gangadean, *Philosophical Foundation*, 133-134.

controls the appetites, there is virtue. Knowledge is virtue. Vice is due to ignorance, for no one errs willingly.

Society is an enlarged version of the individual; it consists of three classes of individuals corresponding to the three aspects of the individual and their virtues. Those whose virtue is wisdom should rule; those whose virtue is courage should be the guardians, carrying out the decisions of the rulers; those whose virtue is temperance should be subordinate to the other two groups. Justice consists in the proper ordering of society. The best society is that ruled by one who knows the good—the philosopher-king. Rule by one for honor or power is less desirable; this is a tyrant. Rule by a few guardians for honor is an aristocracy. Rule by a few for wealth is an oligarchy. Rule by the many according to their appetites is democracy and results in the worst form of injustice, where the order of society is completely reversed.

CRITICAL ANALYSIS OF ETHICAL DUALISM:
Is This View of Good and Evil Justified?

Dualism has an explanation for the problem of evil by locating the problem in the soul becoming involved in bodily existence. Is evil due to the body? There are several problems and/or objections to ethical dualism. 1) If the soul is inherently good, how did it become ensnared in bodily existence? Must there have been a lack (of knowledge) in the soul? 2) If the soul is eternal, how could there be a lack of knowledge in the soul? If the soul grows in knowledge in time and had infinite time, being eternal, how could it have lacked infinite knowledge? 3) If both matter and spirit are eternal, what is the basis for saying one is good and the other evil, as against saying they are merely different? If both matter and spirit are eternal, what is the basis for hoping one can win over the other (as against having an eternal conflict)? 4) Why should the body be considered the source of evil and spirit be considered good? One can conceive of having all bodily needs met and yet have an evil act (as in the Garden of Eden). And one can conceive of a spirit without a body as evil (Lucifer). In these cases, one might think the source of evil is the spirit and not the body. 5) Why should the good be considered the condition of the soul separated from the body, that is, disembodied existence, apart from this world, a state in which the soul exists in a pure contemplative vision of the eternal forms (or in a beatific vision of God)?

THE GOOD:
Plato's View and Possible Reconstruction

Plato's view: The good is not easily knowable or not knowable at all. For Plato, the ascent out of the cave is difficult for anyone. The vast majority do not and cannot make the intellectual journey out of the cave. Since the good is higher than being and truth, it cannot be rationally known. The good as a form is problematic in several ways: As the good is neither virtue nor pleasure, so it is not a form, but an achievement. The good as a form or essence or idea cannot exist apart from things or minds.

Possible reconstruction of Plato's form of the good: The good as a source of the power of knowing and of truth in the forms is the Logos in the mind (reason) and in the (essence) of things. The good as the source of the existence of things is higher than what it causes to exist. It, therefore, would be the Creator. The Logos is the highest being and the source of the intelligibility of being. The acts of a being reveal the nature of that being. God, as Logos, makes his glory known through his actions in creation. It is by reason (logos) that man comes to know the essences of things created, including the good—the end in itself.

RATIONAL PRESUPPOSITIONALISM APPLIED:
Avoiding the Problem of the Forms

Over and against Plato's separation of the forms from the world, there is another way to proceed. Rational Presuppositionalism begins by appealing to certain innate concepts. Concepts are universal in all thinkers. These concepts are about being (whether finite or infinite), existence (whether temporal or eternal), substance (whether matter or spirit), and essences (whether for a class or individual).

By speaking of matter and spirit, one can speak of knowledge and essences. Proceeding this way renders Plato's approach through allegories and the forms unnecessary. Instead, we use reason (logos) to grasp the nature of things that express their essences. The most basic form of being is eternal being; that which is eternal is independent, self-existing, self-maintaining, and self-explaining. An eternal spirit is known by its act of creation. Man, as a rational being is to use his reason to understand the nature of things created. It is by the use of reason through inference from the nature of things that knowledge of essences is grasped. An individual being has an essence that is general for a class (e.g., human nature) and particular for one only (e.g., Socrates-ness). Existence cannot be separated from essence. By understanding essences—the set of qualities that all members of a class have, and only members always have—one understands being and its qualities. It is by understanding through the use of reason that knowledge of being through essences is attained. Thus, by starting with the innate concept of being, one can proceed by rational inference to real knowledge that can be communicated concerning the good and give an account of knowledge as justified true belief. A whole set of basic issues do not come up if we begin first with the concept of being—and then proceed presuppositionally to understand the essences of all being as grounded in spiritual and material substance. Thus, one avoids the pitfalls and metaphysical difficulties inherent in Plato's theory of the forms.

Chapter 8

ARISTOTLE[1]

INTRODUCTION

ARISTOTLE (384–322 B.C.), ALONG WITH PLATO, had a profound influence on Western Christianity. Aristotle directly influenced Thomas Aquinas and, through Aquinas, Roman Catholic theology. He is considered the philosopher/theologian of the Roman Catholic Church. He was a student at Plato's Academy for 19 years. He made a significant contribution to syllogistic logic that we are still able to build upon today, and his work on virtue ethics continues to be influential, especially among Roman Catholic thinkers.

Since Aristotle was a student of Plato, it is natural to ask how he dealt with the shortcomings of Plato's view. A prominent concern for Plato and Socrates was knowledge connected with definitions. To attain knowledge, Plato needed to get concepts into focus. To do so, Plato went in the direction of the forms and the soul.

In metaphysics, Plato speaks about the divine maker and matter; the view is that the forms are eternal. The divine maker is the efficient cause of the world by acting with power to bring the forms into the material world. Why this would be or should be done is not particularly addressed, but is assumed. Did Aristotle see the shortcomings of this dualistic framework, or did he continue to work within that framework?

When one comes to Aristotle, one has to ask to what extent he was engaged in philosophy in terms of the critical use of reason. Did he critically analyze Plato? If so, how far did he get in his analysis? Did he get to the foundational level, or did he only analyze secondary issues?

---

1. For a more concise and refined critique of Aristotle, see Gangadean, *Philosophical Foundation*, 134-136.

The Presocratics did not formulate questions correctly regarding permanence and change, which was one of their primary concerns. Did Aristotle get this problem into focus? Did he improve upon Plato's position in epistemology, metaphysics, or ethics?

As mentioned above, one of the initial points that should be noted about Aristotle is that he made a significant contribution to logic, which is in the realm of epistemology, and what he did has endured. Someone might ask, how could he get things right at the basic level of epistemology and not get less basic things right? We should notice that logic has to have content. What content did Aristotle provide? That is the relevant question, and that is the question that will be examined within the three areas of philosophy.

ARISTOTLE'S PHILOSOPHY:
A Brief Outline

In the realm of epistemology, Aristotle defines knowledge in terms of what is certain and necessary, distancing himself from Plato's theory of the forms. He maintains that all knowledge begins with the senses and that there are no innate ideas. In metaphysics, he describes change in terms of matter taking form, or actuality, and he maintains that what is in a state of potentiality is actualized by the Unmoved Mover (or Prime Mover), which is a version of dependent dualism. In ethics, Aristotle emphasizes practical reason, where knowledge is sought for the sake of action—first in politics (the whole) and then in ethics (the individual).

RATIONAL EMPIRICISM:
Concept Formation, Challenges, and
the Failure to Use Reason Critically

In epistemology, Aristotle did not define concepts as universal and their formation as the first act of reason; minimally, he is ambiguous about whether or not concepts are universal, which is to be expected, given that he attempts to ground epistemology in sense experience, and there are no universals in sense experience. Recall that Plato recognized that permanence is necessary for knowledge. And permanence is not found in the material world; permanence must be beyond the physical world, which is why Plato introduces the forms.

How would one give an account of knowledge with respect to permanence? How does one get these permanent things? Are there forms beyond this world? Is there permanence beyond this world? Is the doctrine of the forms believable? How do we account for permanence without the forms? Must there be permanence for knowledge? Is there something permanent in human beings? Are there essences?

What did Aristotle have to say about essences? He maintained that there are essences, but he also tried to ground knowledge in the senses. Can that be done? If one is an empiricist, one is not going to be able to get to essences. By undermining essence, one undermines permanence, and subsequently, there is no permanence that can belong to a definition. Yet the first underlying point that Socrates was concerned with was finding definitions. One should not yield on denying the reality of essences. The game would be over if there are no essences, for without essences, there is no basis for intelligibility and knowability of the world.

Many followers of Aristotle would say that he is not an empiricist, which is a question to consider. One can certainly say that he shifted from Plato—there is a more rational basis in Plato in terms of sources of knowledge and justifying basic claims. But there is also a commitment to the use of reason in Aristotle—at least in his works on logic. Yet, he wants to assert that knowledge comes through experience by way of abstraction.

Is there a meaningful distinction between empiricism and Aristotle's view? The supposed difference is that empiricists claim all knowledge is through sense experience, while Aristotle says that the mind is merely opened up through the senses. He rejected Plato's forms as the foundation of knowledge and instead turned to the senses. So, whether one says that concepts are formed by the senses, or somehow sense experience gives us the raw data and concepts are abstracted from the data, the shared assumption is that concepts are empirically based. Yet, empiricism does not deliver knowledge.

Consider a few problems with this notion that concepts are empirically based. In the first problem, we can ask, how do you know which particulars to look for in order to derive the concept? Concepts are not formed from a conjunction of particulars. One would not know what to include and what to exclude unless one already has the concept. Someone will object and ask, "Are you saying that we form concepts before we have concepts?" That question seems to presuppose that concepts arise from experience as opposed to an act of reason. Of course, one does not have concepts before one has concepts. The point is about what a concept is and what it is not, and there should be no question that a concept is not a conjunction of particulars; and if concepts were formed through sense experience, then a concept would have to be a conjunction of particulars.

A second problem is, if concepts are empirically based, then (at best) we can only know individual essences. So, even if we did look at particulars, we would have to name each one, and there would be no way to form a universal concept from encounters with particulars (nominalism). The third problem, which is an extension of the second problem, is that if concepts are formed by abstracting from particulars (a conjunction of particulars), then there would be no way to speak about being, causation, essence, substance, or universals. We do not encounter these through the senses. One has never experienced a cause or an essence, but apart from them, one cannot speak of permanence or change, and one cannot speak of a subject that is permanent about which one could have knowledge. Knowledge assumes that there are permanent things about which one can know, and permanence assumes essences, and essences are invisible.

A fourth problem is if Aristotelians try to account for essences by saying, "we just know these things," then this is an indirect admission that concepts cannot be accounted for through sense experience. Rather, "we just know these things" in that our minds are made in such a way that one naturally forms concepts whereby one grasps essences. Thus, the formation of concepts is an act of the mind, not of the senses. Someone will say, "But without the senses, we would have no concepts." There are in fact many concepts that can be formed without any input from the senses (e.g., infinite, eternal, and causation). Moreover, when sense experience is involved in forming a concept (e.g., the experience of a red rose to the concept "redness"), it does not mean that the concepts are abstracted from a multiplicity of particulars.

Does Aristotle affirm what is clear to reason regarding other areas of epistemology? Does he affirm reason as ontological? Reason as a test for meaning? As the same in all persons? Did he engage in the critical use of reason? How rigorously did he apply reason and argument? As one will see with his work in ethics, he did not regard reason as the same in all persons. Aristotle held unexamined assumptions that would have been seen if he was persistently, critically analyzing these things to find meaning. The Book of Hebrews says, God is a rewarder of those who diligently seek him[2]—that is the critical use of reason. Aristotle did good work in some areas. He opened things up in a certain way, but did not press on toward the goal—he was content with positions with which he should not have been content. He was satisfied instead of diligently seeking. Diligently seeking means pressing on all the way to the foundation, not stopping after making some progress here or there. Aristotle begins with what is commonly known (What have the great minds said? What do most people say?) and that would be fine in an ideal world where all sought diligently. But that is assuming that things are as they should be. We do not experience the Fall of man, but does that mean our current state is our natural state? Such a view is naïve; it is reason used uncritically, that is, not at the basic level.

Plato had spoken of knowledge as a kind of perception. He gives various analogies about what it is to know, and it comes down to seeing the light—a kind of perception. Aristotle continues with the idea of perception, but it is through sense experience and what is commonly known to all men. Knowledge is by experience in Plato and in Aristotle. We have noted that no experience is meaningful without interpretation, and that includes the experience that there is an external world. One should not begin with naturally occurring beliefs that spontaneously arise. One should give an account of knowledge. Knowledge is possible by reason and argument.

Plato allows for certain necessary conditions for any dialogue. Both he and Aristotle provide implicit arguments, yet what we do not see is a certain level and process of critique that is systematic in either philosopher. Both present ideas that one must piece together and other ideas that are left unaddressed. What is admirable is that they did engage on a level that is deeper than what is ordinarily done, it was recorded, and it has come down to us. They engaged with some im-

2. *Hebrews 11:6.*

portant questions; however, much was lacking in terms of a systematic approach.

We can conclude our analysis of Aristotle's epistemology by asking, "Where is Aristotle in terms of giving arguments for things that are not self-evident?" He uses or develops arguments, but one does not see much application of these arguments in terms of developing a system of belief. Perhaps we can put it this way: we need a good philosophical foundation, consistently applied, to attain knowledge. Can one say that Aristotelians need to give heed to what is clear to reason? How would Aristotelians reply if asked, can you show that something must be eternal? What would happen if one asked them if we can know this? They might skip to a first cause and the Prime Mover. Is appeal to a Prime Mover the same as saying some things are eternal? Is the Prime Mover eternal? Aristotle and Aquinas rely upon the cosmological argument and not the ontological argument. To get to something must be eternal, the ontological argument must be used. Thus, there are assumptions to be addressed.

QUALIFIED DUALISM:
The Cosmological vs. the Ontological Argument

A basic piece to consider in Aristotle's metaphysics is the Prime Mover. Must there be a first cause? Does Aristotle's first cause argument rule out matter being eternal or the big bang oscillating universe theory? We can reflect on his argument 1) to see whether it is adequate, 2) whether it requires the ontological argument, or 3) if it is reduced to a form of the ontological argument. So, we need to consider the Prime Mover and the dilemma of dependent dualism. Aristotle begins with change, matter, and form. He speaks about actuality and potentiality. He uses the example of an acorn and oak, and then brass and a brass statue. The acorn is potentially an oak tree, and for it to become an oak, it must be acted upon by external forces. The acorn goes through change, but is not the source of change within itself (the sun and water bring about change). Does change seem like a satisfactory explanation? Furthermore, Aristotle says *everything* that has some potentiality must be acted upon by something outside of itself to realize its actuality. To have an actual oak, something must act on the acorn that itself does not undergo change. Otherwise, there would be an infinite regress and no means of explaining change. There must be a source of motion that is itself not acted on by another, and there must be an end to the sequential causes.

The cosmological argument, to show there is a first cause, is different than saying that the physical universe is not eternal. The idea of the Prime Mover does not connect with and set aside matter being eternal and self-maintaining. What does it mean to say that matter has received its actuality from the Prime Mover as the first cause? Aristotle's position is dependent dualism (matter and spirit are both eternal, and matter is dependent on spirit). For what is matter dependent on spirit? Recall the illustration of the acorn. Was the acorn always there or did it become an acorn? One is trying to go back and see if there is something fixed. And one can ask, was there always energy? We can see where this leads. Either matter has some actuality without the Prime Mover, or matter has no actuality without the Prime Mover. This is a contradiction (some and none). If it has some actuality without the Prime Mover, then this is ordinary dualism (vs. dependent dualism). If it has no actuality without the Prime Mover, then this is creation (vs. dependent dualism). In either case, we present an argument against dependent dualism. No actuality means there was actually nothing, and therefore there is nothing there upon which something could be dependent. Questions can be raised to expose the assumptions of dependent dualism.

We are being pushed back to the concept of "eternal." One may not have the basic belief in place because one does not have the basic concept of "eternal" in place. Aristotle did not focus on this basic question. He focused on explaining change in existing things. To focus on the acorn is not to ask whether there is something eternal. This question never occurs to Aristotle because the idea of the order of concept, judgment, and argument is not in focus. One needs to start with the most basic concept and move forward from there. This is consistent with Rational Presuppositionalism. Aristotle does not see the need in general to show that God exists, and he did not see the need to show the clarity of God's existence. The Prime Mover runs into a problem because the categories were not developed well enough between the concepts of matter and eternal.

To motivate persons to engage more critically with Aristotle, one will have to get to the good. Many persons do not see the need for consistent critical analysis of basic beliefs because their view of the good is connected with otherworldliness—heaven as the good. In this view, when one dies, one receives the fullness of the blessing apart from knowing the truth by exercising one's mind in taking thoughts captive. We have affirmed that knowledge is attained by reason and argument, and this is to be applied at the most basic level. Thinking is presuppositional: meaning is understood in light of reason and then truth in light of meaning. From here, other concepts previously mentioned are understood from more basic to less basic. Unless one gets basic things in place, one will not see clarity, and agreement will not be secured. Understanding this is the value that one can take away from a critical analysis of Aristotle's metaphysics.

ETHICS:
The Good, Virtues, and the Existence of the Soul

Moral philosophy is of great interest and is foundational. What is the good? One can be sure that if the foundation of metaphysics is not in place—and this includes what is real and the nature of man—then we will not get far in ethics. Does Aristotle approach ethics as based on metaphysics, which is based on epistemology? Does he acknowledge common ground and the Principle of Clarity as necessary for dialogue? Does he define the good, the end in itself, as distinct from virtue (a means to the end) and happiness (the effect of possessing what one believes to be the good)? If not, what should we expect? We should expect a muddled account of ethics, which is exactly what we get from Aristotle. He did not get the three main categories of ethics into focus. Speaking in terms of our human frailty, one can perhaps applaud him for getting as far as he did (he raises the question, "What is the good vs. means to the good?"). God has compassion for us in our frailty, nonetheless, without faith it is impossible to please God, because he who comes to God must believe that he is and that he rewards those who diligently seek him[3]—not those who causally seek him and do not find him as their reward, but instead find their enjoyment in the creation, rather than in the Creator.

---

3. *Hebrews 11:6.*

A basic question to ask is whether Aristotle or Plato believed in the soul. Rational Presuppositionalism affirms that belief in personal immortality is a necessary condition for morality. Today, many believe that the "mind" is the relation of the parts of the brain, that the mind does not exist. What should one think of the account provided in *The Meno* regarding the slave boy who knows by recollection? In that dialogue, Plato discusses the immortality of the soul. He likens the soul to a finely tuned stringed instrument. We can begin to think about the essence of the soul and the relationships of the forms or the essences. What is the most basic thing you can say about the soul? It is immaterial and therefore not physical. Plato wants to get to the essential characteristic of the soul and says that it is living, yet he does not define the soul as non-extended and conscious. Instead, Rational Presuppositionalism proceeds by noting that it is a given that the kinds of things that exist are either extended or non-extended, non-conscious or conscious. Furthermore, when one says the soul exists, soul should be categorized in those terms. That which seems easy and clear does not come out that way in the Dialogues. One does not see these lines being drawn there.

Does Aristotle say man has a soul? He does not think man has a soul, as does Plato, but rather, he has an active intellect. The active intellect is the aspect of human nature that is rational and grasps concepts. Is the active intellect, which grasps concepts/forms, separate from matter? His doctrine of forms, imminent in matter and different from matter, is a departure from Plato. As one encounters Aristotle, one should note that the basic pieces are not in place. He is not clear about the nature of man and, therefore, man's need. Do all need meaning? Are all humans rational? Aristotle would say that man is a rational animal, but what he means by that depends on the context. Whether all have rationality equally and whether all have the need for meaning is not clear—or how much they need it. Perhaps because of the duality of man's bodily and intellectual existence, he splits the virtues in two—intellectual and moral. It is certainly not true that all humans seek to have truth in place. Aristotle indicates that women tend not to get the truth in place, and the question is whether or not women need meaning. Can everyone attain to the intellectual virtues? We are forced to return to the question: do all people need meaning? Do all need philosophical training in order to find what actually provides meaning?

Moral virtue is a mean between extremes, as bravery is a mean between cowardice and being foolhardy. Moral virtue depends upon training. If there is no moral training, are we held accountable? Is it coherent to say that if you have no possible access to moral training, through no fault of your own, you cannot be moral, but you are still responsible for accessing moral training and being moral? This is not a coherent position. Clarity is necessary for moral responsibility.

One should note that moral virtue is possible without intellectual virtue in Aristotle's framework. In other words, he separates virtue from the good. Yet, these cannot be separated. Moral virtue is a means to the good. Aristotle is not making a clear distinction between talking about what is good—as in *the good*, the source of life and meaning—and talking about what is right and what is wrong. Many people, perhaps most people, do not get clear in their minds what is meant by the end or purpose of life. Ethics is thought of in terms of right and wrong, virtue and vice, and the meaning of our existence is not engaged with. The closest people tend to get is with a future unknown heaven, or Nirvana, or some other mystical paradise that is beyond words. That is the direction that Plato took, and to some extent, Aristotle introduces that idea at the end of his *Nicomachean Ethics*. But this hope does not stand up to critical analysis. We need a hope that is consistent with our nature as rational beings, who have a need for meaningful work and to see continuity between the work we do now and our lives after physical death. Aristotle did not provide us with hope of that sort.

REVIEW AND ANALYSIS:
From the Presocratics to Aristotle

We have seen the Greek philosophers come into difficulty regarding the concept of what is real and that is connected with their not getting to God as Creator and determiner of human nature. They wanted to get to knowledge by getting to permanence. Remember, Plato's forms had to be permanent. The permanence they were concerned with is permanence in the things we normally experience, not in what is eternal. The concern is for permanence in a chair or tree or horse or man. The focus is not on what is eternal, but on permanence. The problem is further compounded by the fact that objects of the senses are not permanent, which leads to the problem of flux and change. Permanence is necessary for knowledge. This cannot be permanence as Parmenides thought, or as in spiritual monism, rather, we need both permanence and change. There must be permanence to the things that are changing. It is necessary that there be both permanence and change as preconditions for knowledge. There must be unity and diversity. We will find this in the more basic—in what is eternal.

There is diversity in being. All being that we know is a unity of diversity. There are more basic concepts behind the philosophers' notions of permanence. For example, substance is more basic and permanent than sense objects. And, when we push back further, we must think about permanence in light of what is eternal. The concepts of eternal, substance, and essences are more basic than the normal objects of the senses that the philosophers were seeking to explain. What we see is that permanence presupposes essence, and both permanence and essences are needed for knowledge.

To get to essence—something that fixes it—you must get to creation. Behind the search for permanence, we have the creation. And there are two types of creation: original and subsequent. Out of the original substance, God separated off things. Original creation was without form and was empty, and God wanted all things to be filled. What is necessary for knowledge of creation is permanence through creation: things that are not eternal, but are nevertheless permanent. We are pressed to the reality of special creation in order to get permanence in things. Original creation is *ex nihilo*. Subsequent creation is forming and filling. Creation, forming and filling, explains permanence in the world. Permanence is by the Logos in the creation.[4] And with the idea of permanence, comes the idea of necessity. The Presocratics, in their pursuit of the logos, were close in their development of logic and the attempt to get to necessary truths. Yet their assumptions held them back from understanding the Logos in its fullness.[5]

The necessity of a statement requires permanence. If it rains, then the ground is wet. It is necessarily the case that the ground is wet when it rains. Wetness is a fixed characteristic of water. It is what

---

4. *John 1:10.*

5. Surrendra Gangadean, *The Word of God: The Logos is Truth* (Phoenix: Logos Papers Press, 2016), Logos Paper No. 30. See: https://thelogospapers.com

makes water, water. Plato's forms attempted to get to necessity and permanence. Much of what Aristotle does is connected with this also. Yet, we cannot merely get to what is permanent, but we must get to what is eternal. Because the philosophers' quest for permanence did not go back to what is eternal, and was not properly formulated, their assumptions and shortcomings led to a host of problems that are still with us today.

In showing what is eternal, and that matter is not eternal and the soul is not eternal, Rational Presuppositionalism avoids many of the disputes coming down to us from Plato. We say that our most basic belief is about our most basic concept. If we do not have a clear idea of essences, lack of clarity contributes to many of the problems in ethics, because good for a being is according to the nature/essence of the being. In addition, the distinctions we made in ethics have kept us from what led to the kinds of problems that Aristotle encountered. In ethics, we gave a more adequate account of human nature, and the good as based on human nature. There may be a difference between male and female, but there is a deeper level of human nature to consider. Similarly, there may be a difference between temperaments, personality, or backgrounds. And, we do not make a distinction between slave or free in the ability to seek the good, as did Aristotle. We preserve the idea that all humans equally have the same nature. We do not view body and soul in tension so as to distinguish between intellectual and moral virtues. Beginning with only some is eternal, creation *ex nihilo*, and each being created after its own kind, avoids many of the problems of the philosophers. Creation provides a basis for permanence. In addition, we affirm the view that words are not simply how we use them conventionally, but words express concepts, which are not conventional, but are universal—they apply to all members of a class of beings and are the same in all thinkers.

These long-standing problems go back to the absence of the doctrine of creation. The ancient writers assumed, without proof, that nothing ultimately came into being or went out of being. They assumed that all is eternal. Why did they begin with this assumption? What reason does one have to believe that all is eternal? Do they think a law of thought is violated if things come into being? Plato and Aristotle made significant contributions to the history of philosophy— contributions that we can and should appreciate—but they never analyzed the system of Greek dualism. They assumed that all is eternal and did the best they could within the limitations of that system. We are not warranted to make excuses for their failure to engage in self-examination at the basic level. Dante may excuse that failure and make these philosophers honorary Christians in his *Divine Comedy*, but we cannot let go of the truth that some things are clear. And when we excuse people for not seeing what is clear, we implicitly deny that it is actually clear, which undermines the claim that all need Christ. If we say that Plato and Aristotle did not sin in failing to know God, then can we claim that it is a sin to fail to know God? If their failure can be excused because they did a pretty good job, then all should be excused; if there is no sin, Christ died for nothing. We can acknowledge that we come short, while also acknowledging that the truth is clear and no one has any excuse for failing to see what is clear, including Plato and Aristotle.

Chapter 9

——

NAGARJUNA AND
MADHYAMIKA BUDDHISM

THE FIRST NOBLE TRUTH OF BUDDHISM is that all is *dukkha*. Interpreted epistemologically, this means that all objects of intellect are empty; they cannot stand up under scrutiny. The intellect gives us discrimination and duality, not reality. The intellect distinguishes *a* and *non-a*, which is interpreted as the source of all duality, division, and discord. Reality, that which can only be directly realized, is calm and blissful, that where all plurality is merged, that where all the cries of the intellect are satisfied.

Nagarjuna (A.D. 150–250) is led to this conclusion by his starting point. He assumes the unity of all being. There is not a distinction between creator and creature. "Never, nowhere, can anything originate," he declares. True creation is impossible, by his analysis of the effect being present in and hence non-different from its cause. Given the unity of all being, all differences are illusory or not ultimate, and hence subject to error when made so by the discrimination of the intellect. *A* is not ultimately different from *non-a*.

Those who persist in the use of intellect come in for scorching criticism:

> Those who are entangled in the meshes of intellect are worse than dogs and they can never know the Real. Just as elephants are stuck in deep mud, so are these fools entangled in language, in letters, words and names. 'Everything has a cause' and 'nothing has a cause'; 'everything is eternal' and 'everything is momentary' . . . all

this is gross and crude philosophy. In real philosophy we have to transcend the categories of the intellect.[1]

What is interesting to note is that the kinds of statements which are opposed are not contradictions, but contraries, both of which may be false. Reality is either all one way or all another way. Nagarjuna does not consider that "some is eternal" and, "some is not eternal." His assumption that all is one, reinforced by his view of the effect being present in the cause, rules that out. Perhaps he legitimately finds both pairs of a contrary false. That, however, says nothing about the ineffectiveness of the intellect to grasp reality, but only that the assumption that all is one (*dukkha* applies to all) leads to the negation of the intellect. It is better to give up one's assumption and to keep the intellect, for in giving up the intellect, one must give up even one's assumption.

A RECENT FORM OF MADHYAMIKA

Attempts have been made recently to apply Madhyamika Buddhism to understanding the history of Western philosophy and, indeed, to dialogue itself within and between all traditions which attempt to understand the world. Ashok Gangadean (1941–) distinguishes the discourse of ordinary or categorical reason and a higher form of reason, transcategorical or meditative reason, which he calls the Logos. He seeks a universal grammar that makes dialogue between worlds possible. The ordinary operations of reason come in for the same condemnation: it is pathological, egocentric, divisive, and destined to doom. Categorical reason cannot grasp the real, the unified field of being, the true Logos.

Transcategorical Reason

Ashok's analysis builds upon Fred Sommers' (1923–2014) analysis of predication, which finds that there is one category by which all predication is unified. One category applies univocally to all that exists. All being is ultimately of one kind. Immediately, we are in the presence of an implicit monism which becomes explicit in due time. The ge-

---

1. Chandradhar Sharma, *A Critical Survey of Indian Philosophy* (India: Motilal Banarsidass Publishers; 1987), 89.

neric problem of (rationality) is this: if mind or voice is situated in grammaticality and is systematically univocal across grammars, *how is inter-grammatical discourse possible?* Inter-grammatical reason necessarily involves some kind of transcategorical or inter-grammatical Univocity—let us call this the "Univocity Condition". In some sense, the Univocity Condition is the Transcendental condition for meaning.

In this reading of reason, which gives us duality and not unity, which gives us *a* and *non-a*, but not the unity from which both must emerge, Descartes' dualism of mind and body is seen as a natural expression from the categorical point of view. Later philosophers struggled to overcome this dualism: Spinoza's monism, Leibniz' spiritual atomism, Hobbes' material monism and Hegel's dialectical idealism—all attempts to overcome the duality naturally flowing out of categorical reason. The infinite is necessarily unified and transcends all limits and cannot be grasped by reason, which necessarily distinguishes and divides and limits.

Ashok's understanding of unity is not a unity of diversity, which affirms the distinctions as necessary for diversity and hence for the unity of diversity. Distinctions must collapse in his view, since distinctions are not distinguished from fragmentation and opposition. Why must man's being be regarded as a dualism to be overcome? Why cannot it be regarded as a unity of mind and body?[2]

An example which he uses to promote the distinction between categorical and transcategorical reasoning is the supposed opposition between the finite and the infinite. This is regarded as a paradigm case of *a* and *non-a*, in which one is excluded from the other. This is seen in the being of Christ who is the Logos incarnate. Ordinary reason cannot grasp the being of Christ. And this transcending category is seen at some point in all worldviews. In all systems, one comes to a unifying category which cannot be grasped by reason.

Categorical Reason Applied to Transcategorical Statements

I think this is too quick and unnecessary a move away from reason, too quick a declaration on the limits of reason. *A* and *non-a* is a for-

---

2. Gangadean, *Philosophical Foundation*, 84-88. See the third argument against materialism for a discussion of the distinction and relation of mind and brain.

mal distinction; they are not necessarily exclusive and opposed. Distinction, yes; opposition, no. The infinite and the finite are distinct, and cannot, and therefore should not, be collapsed into each other. The finite does not include the infinite; but the infinite includes the finite. The inclusion relation is opposed to the exclusion-opposition reading of the relation of the finite and the infinite. A problem was generated where there was none, because of an unnecessary hasty generalization about the relation of *a* and *non-a*. To read *a* and *non-a* as opposition and exclusion is a strawman, which then permits the rejection of reason.

Again, some things which are objectively clear are made obscure by the presumption of the unity of being, a unity which excludes continuing distinctions. It is clear that we are finite beings, and not infinite. On Ashok's view, it is not clear that we are finite. He maintains that we can be infinite and not know it. To be finite is to be fallen, and to be fallen is to be in ignorance, hence we can be ignorant of our infinitude. The three preceding statements are each problematic. Together they are trans-problematic. The first implies that the finite, before it was finite, was infinite. It is the infinite therefore which fell, and therefore it is the infinite which is fallible. But if the infinite is fallible, it is not distinguishable from the finite, and therefore no change or fall is possible. Therefore, neither the infinite nor the finite is fallen, since no fall is possible. The second statement implies that if we are mistaken of some things, we can be mistaken about all things. But universal misunderstanding would collapse all distinctions and in doing so make any utterance impossible and hence make mistakes impossible. The third statement explicitly attributes ignorance to infinitude, since we are infinite and do not know it. If infinitude has any meaning, it cannot be ignorant, for then it knows all and does not know all, at the same time and in the same respect. The only way to avoid what is clear is to deny reason. But this is destructive to our being, since we cannot give up thought. We can only give up our integrity.

Chapter 10

———

AUGUSTINE

INTELLECTUAL JOURNEY

S T. AUGUSTINE OF HIPPO'S (A.D. 354–430) STYLE of philosophizing is personal. It is expressed this way in his *Confessions*. An appropriate means to understanding his position is to follow his intellectual journey. He was brought up by a mother who taught him faith in Christ and the Scriptures. At about seventeen, he questioned his faith and simultaneously yielded to sexual indulgence. What he rejected was an anthropomorphic understanding of the nature of God based on an underlying materialism. He rejected a straw man and turned to Manichaeism in the hope of a more rational view of his faith.

After several years, Augustine saw that the Manichees promised rational explanations were lacking. In leaving them, he once again faced the need for rational support for his belief and engaged the challenge of academic skepticism. At that time, he found a new, more spiritual interpretation of Christianity in Ambrose, the bishop of Milan in Italy, which made use of Neoplatonic doctrine. He went through a crisis conversion and turned to a quasi-monastic form of Christian living. After some years, he became Bishop of Hippo in North Africa. He defended the faith in his writings against Pelagius regarding evil in man and the need for divine grace. His most extensive work was against a pagan interpretation of history in *The City of God*.

DICTUM OF FAITH:
Preliminary Questions

One can see the progression in Augustine's thought throughout his life. The main concern in philosophy is his view of the rationality of religious belief. His view is expressed in the dictum *credo ut intelli-gam*—I believe in order that I may understand. How did this work out in Augustine's life? Can one believe more than one understands or does belief naturally extend as far as understanding extends? Did understanding increase upon belief? Are some things to be believed on the authority of testimony, but others to be believed apart from testimony? Did Augustine work out a consistent view of good and evil? How did he deal with the various encounters in his intellectual journey? Did his faith lead to understanding of why he rejected what he rejected and why he embraced what he embraced?

CONVERSION:
A Dualist Point of View

Augustine abandoned the straw men of anthropomorphism and ma-terialism, but he does not provide a philosophical critique of mate-rialism. The Greek and Roman gods had bodies, and this seemed to carry over into his conception of God in Christianity. In his journey out of Manichaeism and into Platonism, he does not come to terms with the element of materialism present in the dualism on which both are based. He did not come to see that materialism is clearly not to be believed and, therefore, such belief is inexcusable and is therefore a primary expression of moral evil. His turning to Christ was a turn-ing away from sensual indulgence. The voice he heard in the garden, to take up and read, led him to a passage in Scripture which spoke against the sin of sensual indulgence, and this was for him the final turning point. Sin was still defined largely from a dualist point of view, rather than a theistic point of view.

INTELLECTUAL QUEST BOUND BY PLATONISM:
Overlooking Basic Questions

Augustine's reflections were subjectively sufficient for him to take the next step in his spiritual journey, to attain peace of mind, necessary for happiness, yet they do not pass the test for intellectual proof. He rejects Manichaeism for its failure to provide rational explanation for its secondary doctrines, but, not for the logical incoherence of its primary or foundational doctrines of the eternality of matter and souls. The proof for the existence of God, against skepticism, is to show the mind is in touch with something higher than itself, which must be God. Since the mind knows unchanging truths of mathematics, since unchanging truth exists, there is a realm higher than the mind, and what is higher than the mind is God. Plato would allow that the realm of the forms is unchanging, but that is not sufficient to conclude that God exists. For Plato, it required a divine maker to impose the forms on matter, and even then, this is still not the Creator God of theism. These differences at the basic level did not become a matter of concern for Augustine. Faith did not seek understanding at this level. He built on a Platonic foundation, and it left its effect on his world and life view and on the history of Christianity.

UNDERSTANDING OF EVIL

Augustine argued more cogently against Pelagius, a British monk who preached salvation through moral effort, which minimized the need for divine grace. In doing so, he developed the doctrines of predestination, free will, the nature of evil, and the effects of the Fall. Augustine progressed in his understanding of evil, from thinking of it as a material reality (Manichaeism), to thinking of it as the absence of being or a deformity in a being (privation of good), to it being an act of the will which takes pleasure in doing wrong (for example, his stealing of unripe pears from an orchard, when ripe ones were available at home), to seeing it as something transmitted from Adam, the first man, by natural generation (original sin).

FOURFOLD STATE OF MAN:
Doctrine of Grace and Divine Sovereignty

With rhetoric aplomb, Augustine traces the movement of the will of man through four stages of ability, in all of which man remains morally free: before the Fall, man can sin (*posse peccare*); after the Fall, man cannot avoid sin (*non-posse non-peccare*); in the regenerate state, man can avoid sin (*posse non-peccare*); and in the final state of beatitude, man will no longer be able to sin (*non-posse peccare*). A significant distinction between liberty of the will and the ability of the will provided a basis for the later development of the doctrine of grace and divine sovereignty in the Protestant Reformation. However, not recognizing sin as the failure to see what is clear, left room for objections against the teaching of original sin. At best, Augustine's concept of evil was deficient and a source of problems for those he influenced.

DEFICIENT VIEW OF THE GOOD:
Otherworldliness and Its Critics in Modernity

The concept of the good likewise suffers from Augustine's not dealing with basic differences with Platonism. The course of the struggle between good and evil is traced in *The City of God*. It is a struggle that goes on throughout history without good overcoming evil. The reward of the believer is found in the afterlife, in the vision of God, which brings blessedness or full happiness (The Beatific Vision). The vision of God parallels Plato's vision of the good. It is known apart from the material world and the life of the senses. There is in Augustine's teaching an affirmation of fundamental otherworldliness. The creation is not seen as the source of the knowledge of God, to be uncovered through the work of dominion, carried on throughout history by mankind corporately. If one could receive full happiness in the afterlife, there is no necessity for any work to be done here on earth. This otherworldliness is a major rejection of the significance of creation and left the door wide open to the criticisms of Nietzsche, Marx, and Freud. It also allowed involvement with the affairs of the world to be pursued, in reaction, without God, under secularism in the modern world. For Augustine, the good is not the earth being filled with the knowledge of God. The lack of attention to the clarity of general revelation had its effect on his view of the good.

Chapter 11

———

SHANKARA AND RAMANUJA

SPIRITUAL MONISM IS THE ONTOLOGICAL position that there is only one kind of being and that this being is spirit and that all spirit is eternal. Material objects only appear to exist. It is distinct from dualism and from theism.

Points of contact with spiritual monism are reincarnation, karma, yoga, the Hare Krishna Movement, Transcendental Meditation, New Age, and several other instances of Eastern thought. Note that some forms of Indian thought are not monist.

The appeal of spiritual monism is that it is believed to offer an alternative to the emptiness of materialism; it is a hopeful view of the afterlife in which a person reincarnates until enlightenment is achieved; and it is an explanation of why events in this life occur in terms of influence from one's previous lives.

Some objections to reincarnation are that, first, explanation using reincarnation is *ad hoc*—it explains too much. Second, since innumerable lifetimes are involved, the assumption is that knowledge is difficult to attain, yet we suffer until we know. Third, if the soul is eternal, how long has reincarnation been going on—is there real hope that the goal can be attained? And, last, how can a unique event (enlightenment) occur for an eternal being?

Some responses of spiritual monism to these objections are that against the view of a unique beginning or end, the process of reincarnation is cyclical; without beginning and without end. If an endless cycle makes striving for release meaningless, the response is that ultimately the cycle itself is an illusion. Furthermore, if the illusion is inexplicable, then the problem is with reason; ultimately, there is no difference between ordinary existence (samsara) and enlightened existence (nirvana).

There are two forms of spiritual monism. The first is absolute non-dualism, where all is one without parts, called historically *Advaita* Vedanta and espoused by the philosopher Shankara (A.D. 788–820) and in Transcendental Meditation. The second is qualified non-dualism, where all is one with parts, called historically *Dvaita* Vedanta and espoused by the philosopher Ramanuja (A.D. 1017–1137) and in the Hare Krishna movement.

SHANKARA

The central teaching of *Advaita* Vedanta is that *atman* is *brahman*, that the self is the ultimate reality. The nature of *atman/brahman* is pure existence, consciousness, bliss (*sat chit ananda*). That is what the real self is (*tat tvam asi*—that thou art). There is one mind only and its ideas. The world is *Maya* (illusion) or *avidya* (due to ignorance).

Shankara's Views on *Maya* and Brahman

Shankara says that *Maya* or *avidiya*:

> . . . is something *positive* . . . though not real. It is called positive in order to emphasize the fact that it is not merely negative. It has two aspects. In its negative aspect it conceals . . . Reality and acts as a screen to hide it. In its positive aspect it projects . . . the world of plurality on the Brahman-Ground. It is non-apprehension as well as misapprehension.[1]

This quote is important to note for the objection that will be brought by Ramanuja. Shankara says further concerning the world of appearance:

> It is *indescribable and indefinable* for it is *neither real nor unreal nor both*. It is not real, for it has no existence apart from Brahman; it is not unreal, for it projects the world of appearance. It is not real, for it vanishes at the dawn of knowledge; it is not unreal,

---

1. Sharma, *A Critical Survey of Indian Philosophy*, 274.

for it is true as long as it lasts. It is not real to constitute a limit to Brahman and yet it is real enough to give rise to the world of appearance. And it is not both real and unreal, for this conception is self-contradictory.[2]

Again, Ramanuja will use these statements to show the incoherence of *Advaita* Vedanta. Chandrahar Sharma, interpreting Shankara, says:

The words 'real' and 'unreal' are taken by Shankara in their absolute sense. Real means real for all time and Brahman alone can be real in this sense. Similarly, unreal means absolutely unreal like the hare's horn, which this phenomenal world is not. Hence this world is neither real nor unreal. This shows its self-contradictory and therefore incomprehensible nature.... Shankara's intention is perfectly clear – *none can condemn this world as unreal*; he who does it, is *not qualified* to do so and he who is qualified to do so, *will not do so*, for he would have risen above language and finite thought.[3]

A final quote from Shankara will help to illuminate his understanding of ultimate reality.

Brahman is the only Reality. It is absolutely indeterminate and non-dual. It is beyond speech and mind. It is indescribable because no description of it can be complete. The best description of it is through the negative formula of *'neti neti'* or 'not this, not this'. Yet Brahman is not an abyss of non-entity, because it is the Supreme Self and stands self-revealed as the background of all affirmations and denials. The moment we try to bring this Brahman within the categories of intellect or try to make this ultimate subject an object of our thought, we miss its essential nature.[4]

Shankara's statements, and Sharma's commentary, help us to see the metaphysical claims about ultimate reality and the world of appearance assumed in the system of *Advaita* Vedanta.

---

2. Sharma, *A Critical Survey*, 274-275.

3. Sharma, *A Critical Survey*, 279.

4. Sharma, *A Critical Survey*, 280.

The reasons given for belief in *Advaita* Vedanta are based on the analogy of a dream (*Maya* or *avidya*). First, a shared illusion, as in a dream, is not a guarantee of objective reality. Second, in a dream, just because we think we are real does not mean that we are real. Third, as in a dream, there is one self behind the many apparently real selves. Lastly, as in a dream, the only way in which the illusory nature of the individual self and the world can be realized is through mystical experience of self-realization, *samadhi*, enlightenment, awakening.

Objections to *Advaita* Vedanta

The general objection to an appeal to experience for belief is fourfold: First, no experience is meaningful without interpretation. Second, the experience of pure consciousness has been interpreted in many ways and from many worldviews (monist, dualist, Buddhist, theist, etc.). Third, a valid interpretation is internally consistent. Lastly, the interpretation of absolute non-dualism is incoherent in many ways.

Consider the criticisms raised by Ramanuja and the qualified non-dualists. Each question asked illuminates the incoherence of the underlying assumptions of *Advaita* Vedanta. The first question to consider is where does the illusion reside? It cannot be in either Brahman, whose nature is infinite consciousness, or in the individual self, who is part of the illusion. The second question is how can Brahman be concealed given its nature as (infinite) pure consciousness? The third question is how can the world, which is *Maya*/illusion, be neither positive (a thing) nor negative (a thought) nor both nor neither? And lastly, how can the world be neither real (eternal) nor unreal (non-existent) nor both nor neither?

Since Shankara believes all is One and therefore all is eternal, things must be either real/eternal or unreal/non-existent; they cannot be temporal given his assumption. He says that reason cannot grasp the nature of the world as neither real nor unreal. He is faced with giving up his presupposition or reason. He chooses to give up reason. He claims that those caught in the meshes of intellect are like elephants stuck in deep mud. And that the highest philosophy is silence. It isn't is, it isn't isn't, it isn't both, it isn't neither. Silence.

RAMANUJA

Ramanuja developed *Dvaita* Vedanta, all is one with parts, in contrast to Shankara's *Advaita* Vedanta, all is one without parts. Whereas Shankara's view of reality is impersonal (Nirguna Brahman), Ramanuja's view of reality is personal (Saguna Brahman), where we are all part of one personal reality.

Objections to *Dvaita* Vedanta

In Ramanuja's form of non-dualism (one with parts), we are all part of the One (God). What does it mean to be part of the One? There are three possible interpretations to consider. All of the parts are the same, and each is finite. Or all of the parts are the same, and each is infinite. Or all of the parts are not the same; some part(s) are infinite, and some are finite.

There are several objections to qualified non-dualism. The first is that if all parts are finite, then the whole (God) cannot be infinite. Further, beings cannot be finite (growing—going through unique events) and be eternal. The second objection is that if all parts are infinite, each would be complete in itself and, therefore, not have or need parts to make it whole. The third objection is that if some parts are infinite (and eternal) and some finite (and temporal), this would be Creator and creation rather than non-dualism. The followers of Ramanuja, like Shankara and his followers, ought to give up their assumption that all is one.

Chapter 12

AQUINAS

THOMAS AQUINAS (1225–1274) BUILT ON Aristotle as Augustine built on Plato. He affirmed the authority of reason, but saw its limitation with respect to faith. He said, *"the natural dictates of reason must certainly be quite true. It is impossible to think of their being otherwise."*[1] But the truths of reason are not contrary to the Christian faith. He thinks there are truths above reason, to which reason cannot attain. These must be given by special revelation and received by faith. Aquinas conceived of the relation between faith and reason as a synthesis: faith completes reason as grace completes nature. Aristotle is the philosopher of natural revelation, who, in Aquinas' view, accurately read natural revelation. Aquinas, therefore, accepts and builds upon the teachings of Aristotle.

ARISTOTLE'S INFLUENCE

Specifically, Aquinas accepts the rational empiricism of Aristotle in contrast to Plato's pure rationalism. There are no innate ideas; the intellect is opened only from below, through the senses. Therefore, there are no positive, adequate ideas of infinite and eternal, since these are not derivable from the senses. He accepts Aristotle's analysis of change in terms of potentiality and actuality, and form and matter, and along with that, the argument for the existence of the Prime Mover as "what all men think to be God."[2]

Is Aquinas' treatment of the relationship between faith and reason adequate? Does he adequately represent the content of natural reve-

---

1. Thomas Aquinas, *Summa Contra Gentiles*, Book I, Chapter 7.
2. Thomas Aquinas, *Summa Theologiae*, First Part, Question 2.

lation and special revelation and the relationship between the two? Given the differences among philosophers, especially between Plato and Aristotle, does Aristotle adequately read the content of natural revelation? And given the conflicts of interpretation of Scripture, does Aquinas represent the teaching of Scripture in a way that is not contrary to reason? Aquinas makes epistemological claims that are at least problematic. Even if the pure rationalism of Plato is inadequate, the rational empiricism of Aristotle can also be inadequate. In an earlier discussion, Rational Presuppositionalism was offered as an alternative to both Rationalism and Empiricism. That discussion should be revisited.

The particular form of the cosmological argument offered by Aristotle through Aquinas has encountered several objections. The concept of pure potentiality encounters a dilemma: either matter has some potentiality without the Prime Mover, in which case matter is eternal and independent of the Prime Mover, contrary to what both Aristotle and Aquinas would wish to allow; or matter has no actuality without the Prime Mover, in which case, matter is created, contrary to what Aristotle, and Aquinas, who affirms Aristotle, would allow. The notion that there must be a first cause, that there could not be an infinite regress, requires further defense. In the case of the big bang oscillating universe theory, an infinite regress is being affirmed. Unless it can be shown that an eternal process is impossible, there need not be a first cause. There are two ways of doing this: one can show that by its nature, the material world is not self-maintaining, or one can show that the notion of infinite time is impossible. Thomists have done neither of these.

THE FAITH/REASON SYNTHESIS

A further implication of Aquinas' position has been problematic. Since there is no potentiality in the Prime Mover, it must be that the world always existed. To believe that the world always existed and yet was created seems contradictory. Aquinas thought that this paradox was to be overcome by faith. But just at this point, the carefully crafted synthesis between faith and reason begins to break down. Faith intrudes into reason, and faith ceases to be not contrary to reason. It would be easier to think that natural revelation was not adequately read rather than bring in faith to the rescue in a way that destroys both faith and reason.

Aquinas believes that not everyone can see by reason that God exists. Only the few who are skilled metaphysicians can see this. Therefore, the vast majority of mankind must approach belief in the existence of God as a matter of faith and not of reason. So, at best, the faith/reason synthesis, if it works, does so for only a few. Aquinas' position requires one to believe that general revelation is not objectively clear. And this lack of clarity raises the question of whether unbelief in the existence of God is inexcusable. But if unbelief is excusable, then so is all morality, which depends on belief in the existence of God for its rational justification. Aquinas thereby loses the basis for moral evil and, with it, the need for redemption and redemptive revelation. What necessity is there for Scripture? And is one Scripture to be preferred above any other? Why the Scriptures of Christianity and not that of Islam, or that of Judaism, or for that matter any of the Scriptures of the non-theistic religions? In his day, and all the more today, these questions remain pressing.

Not everything that is believed by faith can be said to stand up equally under the scrutiny of reason. There are the mysteries of the Trinity and the Incarnation which may appear to be contrary to reason, but which, in the creedal form in which they have been stated historically, have taken into account common misapprehensions which are contrary to both reason and Scripture. There are the miracles of healing and the resurrection of the dead, which are contrary to the laws of nature, but not the laws of reason and may even be required by reason when the nature of moral and natural evil are considered. There are the miracles of multiplying the loaves and fish and turning water into wine, again, contrary to nature, but not to reason. But there are claims of miracles that may be contrary to reason and nature. And for these, Aquinas cannot maintain that the truth of reason is not contrary to the truth of the Christian faith. This would apply especially to those claims of miracles involving disputed interpretations and which have been the source of division within the community of faith. Some interpretations strain reason to the breaking point when there is no necessity to hold them and a good reason not to hold them. Faith and reason may not conflict, but inadequate interpretations of each may conflict.

THE BEATIFIC VISION:
Man's Highest Good

Aquinas argued for the Beatific Vision of God as man's highest good. He held that "the divine essence cannot be seen by the intellect in any created presentation."[3] This is an implication of empiricism from which the intellect must begin, according to Aquinas. Hence, if God's essence is to be seen, the intellect must see the divine essence itself. "By this vision (seeing God face to face) we are singularly assimilated to God and are partakers of his happiness ... the same happiness wherewith God is happy, seeing himself in the way he sees himself."[4] Aquinas says, "the desire of pure intelligence does not rest satisfied in the natural knowledge which they have of God."[5] But how can we see God as he sees himself? Aquinas says that no created being can, of its natural power, arrive to see God as he essentially is. This implies that by a supernatural act of God, we are brought to see God as he sees himself. Grace completes nature, not just because of the Fall of man, but necessarily, from the beginning of man's creation.

Aquinas' explanation of the good raises questions in three areas. First, why is it not possible to see the nature of God in the things which are created? And if this is thought to be possible, but is considered merely a natural knowledge of God, why is this not satisfactory? Second, is it that all of creation and history reveal the divine nature, but that this is inadequate in that it does not satisfy or is inadequate in that there is more to be known that cannot be revealed by God's works? If the beatifying knowledge is known apart from the creation, what need is there of the creation relative to possessing the good? Seeing that this world is full of pain and sorrow from moral and natural evil, and there is no necessity for this world as far as possessing the good, why go through this vale of history? Why not be created as angels? Third, is it possible for the creature to see God as God sees himself? God's knowledge of himself is necessarily infinite and eternal. Can the finite become infinite in order to see as God sees? And if we do, would there be any essential difference between the creature and

---

3. Aquinas, *Summa Theologiae*, First Part, Question 10.

4. Aquinas, *Summa Theologiae*, First Part, Question 12.

5. Aquinas, *Summa Theologiae*, First Part, Question 12.

the Creator? If we could be made to see infinitely, what need is there to see God rather than ourselves? The qualities of infinite, eternal, and unchangeability are incommunicable attributes. They belong to God alone and cannot belong to any creature.

THOMISTIC NATURAL LAW

Aquinas develops the notion of natural law by asking and answering a series of questions. Is there an eternal law? The answer is yes, if we speak of the law of Reason. Is there in us a natural law? Yes, insofar as reason is in man. Is there but one Divine law? Law may differ as when given to children and to adults. Does the natural law contain several or only one precept? Several. Are all acts of virtue prescribed by the natural law? All. Is the natural law the same in all men? The same. Can the natural law be changed? No. Can it be abolished from the heart of man? No, not the law as a general principle.[6] The questions asked reflect Aquinas' approach to the law. Two things are notable. The law is not grounded fully and firmly in human nature as far as his attempt to justify his answers to his questions. If it were, it would, of course, be the same in all men and unchanging by any understanding of human nature, which is the same in all and unchanging. There is also the question of how human nature is to be understood and whether this conception of man's nature is so clear that the law based on man's nature is incontrovertible so that all can be responsible for its requirements.

A second factor is that the law is conceived as the precepts of virtue, but virtue is understood apart from the good. But more importantly, virtue is not a natural means to the good, understood as the knowledge of God which is infused into man by God. Aquinas is following Aristotle in distinguishing moral virtues and the happiness which comes from intellectual vision. The disconnect between the moral virtues and man's highest happiness raises the question of how moral virtues can be rationally justified. It is difficult to see how Aquinas' notion that virtue is the highest good can be rationally justified given his denial that the basic things are clear to reason. Moreover, Aquinas maintains that (even for the select few who can see what God

---

6. Aquinas, *Summa Theologiae*, First Part of the Second Part, Question 91.

has made known through reason), God has left only a bare revelation of himself, rather than a full and clear revelation, and that is why the source of man's happiness can only be glimpsed in this life. For Aquinas, man's limited knowledge of God at present is not due to sin, which is our fault, but due to our having been created with limited rational faculties, which is God's fault. Thomists may try to hold on to inexcusability by appealing to an innate conscience, but a rational justification for our choices cannot be built upon mere feelings (even if some feelings are widely shared). Following Aristotle, Aquinas tried to establish common ground at the psychological and practical level (i.e., based on immediate experience, common sense, common belief, etc.). He failed to build upon the principles of common ground,[7] so he did not provide a foundation for knowledge.

---

7. Surrendra Gangadean, *Common Ground: The Necessary Condition for Thought and Discourse* (Phoenix: Logos Papers Press, 2016), Logos Paper No. 2.

See: https://thelogospapers.com

Chapter 13

CALVIN

JOHN CALVIN (1509–1564) SHAPED THE THINKING of the Reformed churches in the Protestant Reformation. In the *Institutes of the Christian Religion,* he systematically sets forth his understanding of the Christian faith regarding God, man, salvation, and the church. Of particular concern is his view of the knowledge of God and of the good, which continues the Augustinian view and has influenced a significant segment of Protestant thought.

THE KNOWLEDGE OF GOD:
Sensus Divinitatis

He affirms that the sense of Deity is naturally implanted in the hearts of all men. All men have some idea of the Godhead, which is renewed from time to time by particular experiences. This prevents any man from pretending ignorance and is the basis of man's condemnation when they do not worship and serve God. He also calls this the seed of religion. Even idolatry is ample evidence that the sense of Deity is inscribed in every heart, Calvin thinks. This sense of Deity is by nature and not by nurture. It is not and cannot be imposed by crafty rulers, nor can it be eradicated by any person. Men feel the truth which they desire not to know. Even in scoffing atheists, the worm of conscience, keener than burning steel, is gnawing within them. Try as one might to shake off all knowledge of God, when men's hardness is enfeebled, the sense of Deity is still in vigor. Calvin believes that all are born and live for the express purpose of learning to know God, and if they do not direct the whole thoughts and actions of their lives to this end, they fail to fulfill the law of their being. He cites Plato as teaching this when Plato said that the chief good of the soul consists in resemblance to God, that is, when by means of knowing him, she is wholly transformed into him. Man, through worship of God, aspires to immortality.[1]

Calvin's position on the knowledge of God is ambiguous. He wants to say that all men know God, and yet they do not know God. He wants to say idolatry is evidence that all men know God, yet it is evidence that they do not know God. Is the ambiguity in the word "know" or in the meaning of "God"? If men substitute sticks and stones for God, do they know God? Is worship of Zeus evidence of believing in God? Zeus is finite and came into being. God is infinite and eternal. Is Plato's divine maker God? God is supposed to be the Creator of all things, of matter, and the souls of men; Plato's divine maker is neither. Here Calvin, along with Augustine, showed an uncritical acceptance of Plato and thereby showed a lack of attention to the most basic attributes of God. Plato lacks knowledge of God, as do believers in Zeus, and worshippers of sticks and stones. It is puzzling, therefore, for Calvin to claim that all men know God, and cite idolatry as evidence of this. One would conclude the opposite if understanding of basic attributes of God were a necessary part of knowledge.

Calvin maintains that though the seed of religion is in all men, few cultivate it so that hardly anyone has knowledge of God. Suppose we say the sense of Deity is the very most rudimentary element of knowledge of God and that this is what all men have. The question arises, what is to be included in this minimal knowledge of God? Since this knowledge is what leaves men inexcusable, what is the minimum for inexcusability? Since idolaters, too, are inexcusable for idolatry in Calvin's view, they must lack the minimum knowledge. If this is so, Calvin cannot cite idolatry as evidence that all men know God. Idolaters appear to be acting on what they believe when they bow to their god. They cannot be faulted for their practice. If they are to be faulted, it must be for their belief which comes short of what they ought to know.

Calvin seems to equate the seed of religion, the sense of Deity, and having knowledge of God. He is operating with the definition of religion as belief in a deity, however crude. On this view, forms of

---

1. John Calvin, *The Institutes of the Christian Religion*, trans. and ed. Ford Lewis Battles (Grand Rapids, MI: W.B. Eerdmans, 1987), Book 1, Chapter 3.

Buddhism, Hinduism, and Taoism would be excluded as religions, as well as explicit antitheists and pure naturalists, including secular humanists. But if theistic belief is religious, so is atheistic belief, because they function formally in exactly the same way. Both are used to give meaning to experience, so both are equally religious. In this way, all men, needing meaning, and giving meaning to their life, are religious, unlike non-rational creatures. All men have the seed of religion as a formal feature of their being as rational beings. But being religious does not require belief in a higher power or a deity to which he bows. In Hinduism, the self is the highest power. Atman is Brahman. Man, in his true self, is the divine being. The seed of religion should not, therefore, be equated with the sense of deity.

Believers in a higher power may be said to believe in a deity, but not necessarily. While Zeus is a higher power, he is not the highest power, being born of another and therefore dependent on what is higher. Perhaps this realization led Thales to look beyond the gods for the explanation of how things are in the universe. There are principles higher than the gods, to which they, too, must eventually bow. Belief in higher powers is not sufficient for belief in God nor for the knowledge of God. What is necessary for belief in God is belief in a higher power than which none is higher, and which is above all others; else, it would not be a higher power. The sense of deity should not, therefore, be equated with having knowledge of God. An idolater believes in a higher power than himself, but not in the highest power, and therefore not in God. The sense of Deity understood in this way is not evidence for all men having knowledge of God. The highest power is not a higher power merely.

Calvin does not consider that while belief in God may not be imposed from outside, the existence of the belief may be explained naturally apart from implying the existence of God. Freud, for example, suggests a spontaneous belief in God arising from infantile dependence, neurotically projected and mixed with fear and guilt based on oedipal impulses naturally occurring in man. Calvin likewise suggests, while referring to Plato, that the knowledge of God is naturally transformative, yet he also suggests that man often suppresses this knowledge of God so that this knowledge is not naturally transformative. This view has left a long history of voluntarism in Christian thought, in which the will is seen as acting independently of and in opposition to the intellect.

THE KNOWLEDGE OF GOD AND THE GOOD

There are other ambiguities in Calvin regarding the good. At times the knowledge of God is the good, but this knowledge is not the knowledge of God which is to fill the earth. For Calvin, heaven is man's home; this earth is a place of exile. Leaving this world means entrance into real life, in comparison with which this world is but a grave, a vestibule. Calvin may share the common assumption of Christianity in his time that direct knowledge of God (the Beatific Vision) apart from God's self-revelation of himself through his work of creation and providence (history) is the goal, consistent with the Platonism on which Augustine built. At times he may think of the goal as the removal of the natural evil of death, as when he says that through worship of God, man aspires to immortality.

These critical observations do not nullify much else in Calvin's work. But they point out the uncritically held assumptions that Calvin shared with others in the Christian tradition up to that time and the need to examine assumptions if the problems of reason and skepticism are to be resolved. The progress in examining assumptions is part of the intellectual work that goes on in history, even when it goes on through much pain and sorrow because it progresses so slowly. This is not a denial of the work which others have done, but a call to finish the work which they have begun.

Chapter 14

———

RATIONALISM

THE RATIONALIST PHILOSOPHERS SOUGHT knowledge through reason. History shows that they did not succeed. Is that because reason is insufficient for knowledge or because they used reason insufficiently? Current philosophical lore has it that reason cannot get us to knowledge in light of the failure of the Rationalists. I believe that the Rationalists failed to use reason sufficiently. In what follows, I will try to illustrate how this is so.

DESCARTES

René Descartes (1596–1650) sought, through radical doubt, to establish the foundation for knowledge by believing only those truths that are known clearly and distinctly. The senses, he saw, could be easily doubted, as well as memory beliefs and even beliefs about mathematics. A powerful demon could so affect his mind that he could be deceived. But even if he was deceived, he was still thinking, albeit falsely. And thinking required a thinker. He could not doubt his existence when he thought he was thinking. And, he believed, he knew immediately that he was thinking. He concluded with his famous foundation for all certainty: *cogito ergo sum*—I think, therefore I am. This was true whenever he thought it and could not be doubted.

Descartes leaves open the nature of the "I," which is doing the thinking; he does not settle whether this "I" is the mind or the brain. Neither does he settle the relation of the self to the external world. The *cogito* does not seem sufficient as a foundation on which to build the whole structure of knowledge. As a matter of fact, the truth of the *cogito* itself may be called into doubt and has been, in some lines of thought.

The school of Indian philosophy known as *Advaita* questions the existence of the self as we are aware of it, which is the phenomenal self. Using the analogy of a dream, it is possible to think one exists, in a dream, without actually existing at all. Just as there are many dream figures in one's dream, each of whom thinks that he exists, so there are many persons now who share a common world, all of whom are in the mind of another. Only this Other truly exists. The immediate experience of self-existence, or of appearing to think, is not indubitable. No experience is meaningful without interpretation. And there are several interpretations of self, each of which must be tested for meaning. Clarity from experience is not the clarity of the laws of reason, which cannot be doubted. Descartes did not notice the assumption which he used to interpret his experience, namely that appearance (in the experience of the "I think") is reality.[1]

It also needs to be shown how the self cannot be the brain, from an understanding of the nature of a physical activity and a mental activity, in order to establish the existence of the self as mind or soul or spirit or consciousness, or that which is unextended. To get to the external world, it will have to be shown how one's mind or another mind is not the cause of what is seen. This has been done earlier.

Descartes encountered the problem of relating the mind to the body and offered an explanation which was unsatisfactory. The difference between the two substances of the mind and the body was so great as to leave little room for a satisfactory explanation. Berkeley and Leibniz both offered explanations that were unsatisfactory in other ways. However, the problem may lie in the nature of explanation itself, conceived in causal terms. The question appeared to be how two things of radically different types—mind and body—can have any effect on one another. The question rather is what is the nature of causal explanation? In causal explanations, complex causes are broken down into simple causes. But simple causes cannot be broken down at all. They simply are, whether between substances of two entirely different sorts or between substances of the same sort. And since simple causal

---

1. Gangadean, *Philosophical Foundation*, 112-114. Here, it has been shown how *Advaita* has to deny reason in trying to maintain its position.

connections are not observable, they must be a necessary requirement of reason in thinking about the world.

Descartes' proof for the existence of God is a version of the ontological argument. He argues from the necessary existence of an idea to the external world by way of trying to account for the existence of such an idea. He thinks since he could not be the source of the idea of the infinite, given the finitude of his being, that an infinite being must be the origin of such an idea. It may appear, therefore, that he thinks that he can be the source of the idea of the finite, but not of the infinite. Again, a sort of empiricism is assumed to be the basis of this idea. But if one has the idea of the finite, by reason, necessarily, one has the idea of the infinite, for in conceiving of anything as *a*, the mind simultaneously conceives of *non-a*. Since these concepts are logical complements, if one is possible from oneself, then the other is also possible from oneself, and no appeal to God is necessary to explain the origin of the idea.

SPINOZA

There has always been a problem in describing the basic features of the universe. Specifically, there have been distinctions made implicitly between substance, being, and property. Aristotle conceived of substance as a being. Baruch Spinoza (1632–1677) conceived of being as substance. Commonly, substances have been conceived as spirit or matter, which may be, in turn, conceived as temporal or eternal, infinite or finite. Perhaps the way in which the distinctions may best be understood is in their relation to properties. Each substance has different kinds of properties. Properties may be properties of substance, of a being, or of other properties. Properties of substance belong to many beings of the same kind and to all parts of each being of a kind, where it makes sense to speak of parts. Properties of a being belong to that being alone or to that kind of being. Then there are properties of properties, whether belonging to substances or to beings.

Spinoza's analysis of substance led him to the conclusion that there is only one substance, and that substance is God. How did he reach this conclusion? Can it be avoided? I will note some of his axioms, definitions, and propositions and comment on alternatives that these disallow and why.

Axiom 1. Everything which exists, exists either in itself or in something else.[2]

No distinction is being made here between substance and a thing. Properties exist in things, but beings do not exist in substance in the same way as properties exist in things.

Axiom 2. If a thing can be conceived as non-existing, its essence does not involve its existence.

For Spinoza, there is one substance, God, and God exists necessarily. So, in an important sense, there should be nothing that could be conceived as non-existing. Yet he relies on our commonsense notion, which allows some things (perhaps even substances) that can be conceived to be non-existent.

Definition of 'substance': that which is in itself and is conceived through itself (that of which a conception can be formed independently of any other conception).

In an important sense, both being and substance can be said to exist in themselves, in contrast to properties, which cannot be conceived to exist apart from being or substance. This definition does not allow for this distinction of a being from substance.

Definition of 'attribute': that which the intellect perceives as constituting the essence of a substance.

No distinction is made between the attribute of a substance and the attribute of a being. Furthermore, there are essences of beings that do not imply the existence of these beings, for example, the essence of a tree or rock.

Definition of 'mode': the modification of substance, or that which exists in, and is conceived through, something other than itself.

Spinoza sees particular beings as modifications of substance. A tree is a modification of the substance of matter. At times, however, he sug-

---

2. Benedict Spinoza, *The Ethics* (Indianapolis: Hackett Publishing Company, 1992).

gests that matter and spirit are themselves modes and not substances. He cannot distinguish the modification of a substance (matter/tree) from the modification of a being (acorn/oak).

Definition of 'God': a being absolutely infinite—that is a substance consisting in infinite attributes.

Here Spinoza explicitly uses being and substance interchangeably, something not commonly done and therefore warranting explanation, which is lacking. Further, what it means to say that God has infinite attributes, and if that is possible, and whether it is necessary to claim that, needs explanation. Is God both finite and infinite? Is God both wise and unwise? Must God be both spirit and matter in order to be infinitely wise? Would any perfection be lacking in God if he did not possess all actual and possible attributes?

Proposition 5. No two substances can have the same attributes.

Here it needs to be made clear whether all attributes are attributes in the same sense, since Spinoza elsewhere distinguishes substances from modes and allows modes to have attributes. It must also be clear whether substance and attributes are identical or whether attributes exist in substance, but may exist in more than one substance. This leads Spinoza to the conclusion that there is only one substance, namely God.

Proposition 7. Existence belongs to the nature of substance.

On the face of it, it appears that matter does not have to exist at all or for that matter, to exist eternally. But if matter is a mode of substance, and extension belongs to matter as the mode and not to substance, substance has no attributes, and becomes an unknown and unknowable.

Proposition 11. God or substance, consisting of infinite attributes, necessarily exists.

That would follow from the definition of "God" and proposition 7. But these have already been commented on.

Proposition 14. Beside God, no substance can be granted or conceived.

This implies there is one substance only. Even if God had all attributes, it is still possible to have another substance with some of the
attributes and, therefore, different from one having all attributes.
Spinoza's claim need not be granted. Many have conceived of other
substances besides God. Matter for example, and other spirits have
commonly been conceived as other than God.

How is it that Spinoza came to hold a pantheistic view of God, in
singular contrast to the Judaic tradition in which he was brought up
and from which he differed to the point of lifelong excommunication?
Did reason require this from him, as he seemed to think? Certainly,
others with equal passion and claim of rationality have held contrary
positions, including anti-theists. Whatever personal factors moving
him to do so, and whatever subjective claim to rationality, his view
of what it means to affirm the infinitude of God, and the distinction
from the substance of a being were not subject to rational scrutiny by
him. The failure to critically examine his assumptions on these points
led him to conclude with a pantheistic conception of God. Not reason, but the failure to use reason is the source of this difficulty.

LEIBNIZ

Gottfried Wilhelm Leibniz (1646–1716) argued that this is the best
of all possible worlds. This was a necessary implication of belief in
an all good and all powerful God. Voltaire satirized this view in his
novel *Candide* by showing a series of calamities that human beings are
subject to. Leibniz's rational inference is opposed by Voltaire's *tour de
force* through human experience, and sympathy seems to be won over
by Voltaire. Does the problem of evil make it unclear that God exists?
This is a long-standing and ever-recurrent problem for theists and one
of the ongoing sources of skepticism. It raises questions against theism, and in Leibniz, it raises questions against rationalism and reason.

Several points in Leibniz contribute to the vulnerability of his theodicy. He argues from the interconnectedness of all things to this being the best of all possible worlds. "If the smallest evil that comes to
pass in this world were missing in it, it would no longer be this world,

which with nothing omitted and all allowances made, was found the best by the creator who chose it."[3] But interconnectedness is not sufficient to explain evil. There could be interconnectedness without evil. While evil is part of the concept of this world, this does not of itself argue that there could not be another world, better than this one, without any or as much evil. Further, the concept of a world does not entail the concept of evil. And, on interconnectedness, since Leibniz's monads are in a preestablished harmony, and not causally connected, there appears to be no sufficient reason for having harmony established one way rather than another.

Leibniz makes several standard appeals, all of which have been addressed elsewhere (see Hume's *Dialogue Concerning Natural Religion* on the problem of evil). Evil originates, he says, in the nature of the creature. Since man is finite and cannot know all, he can deceive himself and commit other errors. Here he argues from possibility to actuality without grounds and without giving consideration to the move from actuality to necessity. He argues, with the Schoolman, that the formal character of evil has no efficient cause, for it consists in privation. Yet this cannot mean that evil is without cause. He argues that God permits evil and that he is earnestly disposed to save men to prevent damnation if there were not some stronger reason to prevent it. But the reason is not suggested. What he does state is that the moral goodness of God is such that the world was created with the happiness of humans in mind, and this is specifically rejected by Hume and Voltaire in different ways. He adds that evil often serves to make us savor good the more, a position that confuses variety (which enhances satisfaction) with opposition (which hinders satisfaction).

In characteristic fashion, neither Leibniz nor his critics examine the assumptions about the nature of good and evil when discussing the problem. Specifically, what is the relation between natural and moral evil, and what is the nature of moral evil? Is clarity of general revelation necessary for the possibility of moral evil? Is the root of evil failing to see what is clear, including seeing the nature of evil? Then, ironically, the problem becomes: due to evil in me, I cannot understand why there is evil in the world.

---

3. Gottfried Wilhelm Leibniz, *Theodicy* (Whithorn: Anodos Books, 2017), 39.

Chapter 15

———

EMPIRICISM

E MPIRICISM IS THE MAJOR ALTERNATIVE in epistemology to ratio-nalism. It maintains that all knowledge is from sense experience. Some forms of empiricism are radical, extending the scope of experience beyond the senses to include mystical experience. Specifically, empiricism denies the existence of innate ideas, ideas which were not ultimately derived from experience.

LOCKE

In John Locke (1632–1704), the originator of empiricism in the Modern period, the mind is conceived as a blank tablet (*tabula rasa*) upon which the senses leave impressions. The implications of Locke's empiricism were worked out by George Berkeley (1685–1753) and David Hume (1711–1776) in ways Locke would not have anticipated, and which he would have avoided at all costs.

The appeal of empiricism is that it is close to common sense, which most men readily assent to. It has a pragmatic quality, which resists speculation and critical thinking, and gravitates toward surface-level thinking (literalism). The world is the way it appears. There are rocks and trees and stars and human beings who are as they appear to the senses. The visible world is the real world; the invisible world is hardly real. The world that is revealed by the senses is believed in spontaneously, effortlessly, with common consent. The invisible world is a matter mostly of speculation, filled with interminable, tedious disputes. Furthermore, empiricism is the assumption of science, the world we have learned to depend upon for real discoveries and progress in the things of life which affect us most tangibly.

The notion of innate ideas, which Locke explains away, needs clarification. Some examples of innate ideas would be the idea of cause and effect, of substance, the truths of mathematics, and the laws of thought (identity, non-contradiction, and excluded middle), as well as concepts of infinite and eternal. What characterizes innate ideas is their necessity. They are necessary in two ways: some are necessary for the possibility of thought, and to deny them is to deny the possibility of thought, and some are necessary in that their contradiction is not possibly true. Locke operates with another view of innate ideas, as originating from one use of reason, which leaves it open to some of the objections he raises. What is at stake in the argument is the possibility of certitude. Hume has shown that if all knowledge is from sense experience, there can be no certitude. The consequence of empiricism, when held consistently, is total skepticism.

Locke's first objection is that innate ideas such as "what is, is," and "it is impossible for the same thing to be and not to be" are not universal as innate ideas are supposed to be. Most human beings do not know these, particularly children and idiots. He argues that ideas cannot be innate without being known, and if so, then there is no way to distinguish innate from acquired ideas. "Not innate without being known" seems to have a model of sense impression as the paradigm for knowing. Even children and idiots have awareness of sense impressions when they occur. But to use a response often used by Locke himself, this seems too frivolous a position to merit an answer.

An alternative view of innate ideas is that by the use of reason, they come to be known. They are, like the truths of math, not known from birth, but come to be known by the use of reason. Here, Locke conceives of reason as that by which we "deduce unknown truth from principles or propositions that are already known."[1] Since there are no truths known from birth, all must be discovered. But discovery is made from things already known, in Locke's view. And since all must be discovered, nothing can be discovered, seeing that there is nothing known from which discovery can be made.

The answer to this dilemma is to assert that all innate ideas are not deduced, that the laws of thought themselves are not deduced, but

---

1. John Locke, *An Essay Concerning Human Understanding.* Edited by Peter H. Nidditch (Oxford: Clarendon Press, 1975), 51.

that by which deductions are made. Locke asks, "how can it with any tolerable sense be supposed, that what was imprinted by nature, as the foundation and guide of our reason, should need the use of reason to discover it?"[2] Here Locke does not distinguish the constructive use of reason, the foundational belief upon which reason makes inferences, and reason itself, which makes any thought possible. As a result, he finds this interpretation of innate ideas unacceptable.

A third objection he offers is that the coming to the use of reason is not the time we come to know these maxims, that we come to the use of reason before the maxims are known. He says: "Illiterate people and savages pass many years, even of their rational age, without ever thinking of this and the like propositions."[3] He adds that even if they were at the same time, one would not be the cause of the other, but that they would be merely concomitant. These propositions are, or are closely connected with, the law of identity and the law of non-contradiction. Now, it seems entirely possible to have assumptions without being aware of having assumptions. And it is possible to do something without being aware that one is doing it (using one's reason) or being able to explain how it is that one is doing it. People use reason long before they come to recognize the laws of reason as such. Since the knowledge of the laws of reason are abstracted from the use of reason, the use must necessarily precede knowledge of it. We use concepts long before we learn to define them, and both the educated and the uneducated use concepts, but struggle to define them.

One last objection will be considered here. Locke draws a close connection between the use of reason to form general ideas and knowing the use of general terms. Our first ideas, he observes, are from our most common impressions. A child knows the difference between sweet and bitter, and these are among its earliest ideas. Since these ideas are clearly based on experience, we have reason to expect that all our ideas are based on experience. It can be granted that our earliest ideas are empirically based without denying that some ideas are innate, particularly the laws of reason. If ideas are distinguished from images or impressions of senses, and if ideas are general, not attached to particulars, and if ideas necessarily distinguish *a* from *non-a*, then the

---

2. Locke, *An Essay Concerning Human Understanding*, 51.

3. Locke, *An Essay Concerning Human Understanding*, 52.

laws of reason are at work in the formation of our very first idea and not something which subsequently arises, possibly from experience.

These reflections on Locke help us to see how important it is to have a clear idea of what reason is before we begin to undertake a critique of it. This is true of all critical discussions. We must begin with what is more basic. And in all discussions, meaning is more basic than truth. We must know what reason means before making any judgments about it. And clearly, the most basic thing to be said about reason is that it is the laws of thought by which concepts, judgments, and arguments are formed.

BERKELEY

Berkeley developed the implications of Locke's empiricism and concluded that what we can know to exist by experience are minds and their ideas. There is no knowledge possible of a material world based on sense experience. To be is to be perceived—*Esse est percipi*. This conclusion has been scoffed at or ignored, but it has not been answered. How did he come to this conclusion, and can it be answered?

In *Three Dialogues Between Hylas and Philonous*, Berkeley argues that since sensible things are things immediately perceived by the senses, and what is immediately perceived by the senses is in the mind, then sensible things are in the mind. For example, since an intense heat immediately perceived is experienced as nothing other than pain, and pain is in the mind; therefore, intense heat is in the mind. Berkeley is careful to distinguish what is thought and what is immediately experienced. Thinking about heat is not the same as experiencing heat. One may think of intense heat by inferring it from a mild degree of heat understood to be experienced some distance away from the intense heat. But that is to think of the cause of the mild heat and not experience the intense heat itself. What is immediately experienced is the mild heat; what is thought is intense heat. And experience is not thought. To consistently base all knowledge on sense experience—as Locke does—requires the distinction between thought and experience and, therefore, the conclusion that what is known by sense experience is in the mind.

To illustrate further, it is commonly joked that if a tree falls in a forest and there is no one there to hear it, does it make a sound? The answer, for Berkeley, is no. Sound is the effect of sound waves on an ear. If there is no ear present, then there are sound waves, but no sound. We think of sound waves, but we immediately perceive sound. There is a difference between the cause of what I hear and its effect, which is what is heard. The effect comes through the senses, and the cause is known apart from the senses. But, if we have no knowledge apart from sense experience, then we cannot really speak of sound waves as the cause.

Furthermore, the idea of substance—as a material substratum in which qualities perceived are supposed to inhere—is not an idea based on any sense experience, since the substratum is itself devoid of all sensible qualities. It is an unknown and unknowable in empirical epistemology and, as such, should be abandoned. To suggest the substratum has the primary qualities of extension and shape devoid of the secondary quality of color is to reintroduce an unknown, since we can have no experience of size and shape without color. It, therefore, cannot be said that by material world is meant a material substratum having only primary qualities. For Berkeley, the idea of a material world must be abandoned, since we have no idea or experience of it.

What, then, is the cause of what is seen? Allowing the idea of causality for now, and allowing the absence of the external world, Berkeley concludes that the cause of what is seen is not the material world, but is spiritual, that is, God. It is not the self that is the cause of what is seen because the common agreement in experience cannot be explained. Furthermore, a spiritual cause of what is seen avoids the vexing problem of the relation of the mind and the body, left over from Descartes. Hence, he concludes that God and minds exist, and that God is the cause of the ideas in our minds.

The conclusion that God is the cause of the ideas in our minds is not warranted if there are ideas of reason apart from the senses. Allowing this, it can be argued that the cause of what I see is neither my mind nor God's mind, but is outside all minds. If my mind were the cause of what I see, I would have total control of what I see. Since I do not have total control, the cause is not my mind. If another mind were the cause of what I see, then I would have no control whatsoever. But I do have some control—I can decide within limits what will appear next in my field of vision, for example, the floor or the wall, whereas if another mind were the cause, I would have no control, even as one has no control in watching what comes next on a screen in a cinema. Since the cause of what I see is neither my mind nor another's mind, the cause must be outside all minds. And what is outside all minds is called the material world. Hence one need not fall prey to Berkeley's philosophical idealism. But neither is it sufficient to scoff at it or to ignore the position.

HUME

David Hume has been considered the skeptic *par excellence*. He has questioned the rational justification for the foundational ideas of causality, morality, the self, and religion. He has done so by extending the logical implications of empiricism which Locke began and was developed by Berkeley. One can agree with the validity of his arguments, but question their soundness.

Causality

One can agree with Hume's observation that causality is not an observable phenomenon. Hume tries to explain on empirical grounds how we come to the notion of causality. The constant conjunction of two events creates in us the habit of expectation by which we expect one event to follow upon the other. There is no necessity that one event follows the other. Insofar as there is a sense of necessity concerning the connection of the two events, this can be accounted for by the habit of expectation. Take away causal connections in the world, and all science and metaphysics collapse. We are plunged into skepticism, which, according to Hume, is the only honest position.

If Hume meant that there can be uncaused events, or that some events are uncaused, or that no event is caused, then the intelligibility of the world, including the thought process, collapses. One's thoughts are not caused by anything in the world: neither impressions nor judgments. Reasons are not causes for the thoughts of a rational being. Our nature does not cause any need in us. There can be no distinction between meaning and gibberish, since all are equally uncaused. This would apply to any remark of Hume, and so his position would be self-refuting. In truth, we could not even speak of Hume as having a position in the sense that there is no causal connection between the sounds which appear to emerge from near Hume's mouth and anything Hume did to produce that sound. Without cause, nothing can be produced.

If Hume meant that we cannot know by experience the principle of causality, then this can certainly be granted and overcome by saying that causality is a requirement of reason and, along with the laws of reason, is a necessary condition for thought. This is to relocate the necessity of causality from a particular relationship between two things to a transcendental necessity at the level of principle for the intelligibility of the world in the occurrence of every event.

If Hume meant that we cannot know in any particular instance that one thing is the cause of another, that the idea of an effect is not contained in the idea of it so as to be rationally deducible from the idea of the cause, this can be granted. Experience is necessary to know what causes what, although experience is not sufficient to conclude what is the cause of an effect in any case. But there is a world of difference between saying that we cannot be sure what the particular cause may be and saying that there is or may not be a cause operating in any or all instances of change.

Moral Judgments

Hume questions the rationality of moral judgments in two ways. First, he notices the distinction between judgments of fact and judgments of value and that value judgment about what ought to be done cannot be deduced from any fact. There is a logical gap between "is" and "ought," which cannot be filled by reason. Secondly, he maintains that "morals excite passion, and produce or prevent actions. Reason of itself is utterly impotent in this particular. The rules of morality, therefore, are not conclusions of reason."[4]

It is true that bare judgments of fact do not give rise to judgments of value. For example, we may agree that someone took their life, but disagree whether it ought to be done or not. And we may agree that dropping a nuclear bomb will kill two million people, but disagree on whether or not we ought to drop the bomb. There is a gap between a bare "is" and an "ought." However, the question is whether we base

---

4. David Hume, *A Treatise on Human Nature* (New York: Oxford University Press, 2001), 295.

moral judgments on bare matters of fact or whether we base judgments on interpreted facts. Hume's empiricism inclines him not to
notice that data coming through our senses are interpreted. If a person
takes "his own life," and this is understood in an absolute sense, that
his life belongs to none other than himself, that his life not only does
not belong to any other human being, but also that his life is not a gift
from God, then suicide is morally permissible. But if his life is given
to him by God, and it is not his own to dispose of as he wills, then
suicide is not morally permissible, on the face of it. Whether one's life
is one's own or given by God is not a moral judgment, but a matter of
fact depending on the "is" of God's existence and being the Lord and
giver of life. Hume blithely avoids considering this sense of "is" and,
therefore, raises up an objection that is really irrelevant.

Again, is it true that judgments of reason do not excite the passions,
and therefore morality is not a matter of reason? Hardly. Hume's empiricism causes him to regard judgments of reason as based on sense
impressions only, a position which cannot be taken seriously. It seems
that it is a judgment of reason that we are rational by nature in that
we make true or false judgments using the laws of reason. It also seems
a matter of reason that the good for man, that is, what is sought for
its own sake and not for the sake of another, is based upon human
nature, that the good for man as a rational being is the use of reason
to the fullest, that is, that the good is knowledge.

Now perhaps Hume may grant that this is the good and ask why
should I seek the good? The question may be taken in two senses: why
should I seek anything, good or evil, or why should I seek the good
over evil? To the first, it may be answered that as a living human being,
I cannot avoid seeking or choosing. I cannot choose not to choose.
Even suicide, or not thinking, is a choice. To the second, it may be
asked whether I am choosing evil to be my good or whether the choice
of evil as self-destructive is chosen with that understanding and without any other misunderstanding. What distinguishes choice from a
mere event is deliberation. And deliberation involves the understanding. One cannot deliberately misunderstand, although one may refuse
to seek understanding. To call good evil is to misunderstand. And to
choose is to choose for the self and assumes the self, and there cannot,
therefore, be a choice of evil without misunderstanding, which is destructive to the self.

Now, as to whether the understanding excites the passion or whether it is sufficient to do so, we can consider the following. Passions such as fear, and love do not arise from the understanding, but are directed by the understanding. We may consider that the passions are already in existence, waiting for an object to present itself. The passions are not brought into existence, but are already in existence, like our capacity to taste. The awareness of the passions arises when an object is presented, with some judgment regarding its relation to what is considered good. Passions are never objectless. We never fear in general, but fear is the response to what we think threatens our possession of the good. And the object in relation to the good is always presented by the understanding. Therefore, the understanding is not only necessary, but is sufficient to excite the passions. And the understanding and the passions are sufficient to move us to action. Bare understanding without any relation to the good is not able to excite passion, but understanding which interprets objects of experiences in relation to the good, does naturally excite passion. Since understanding the good is based upon reason, moral distinctions (contrary to Hume) are derived from reason.

Objections to the Rationality of Belief in God

Hume has objected to the rationality of belief in God in two ways: first, from the problem of evil, and second from the irrationality of belief in miracles. After setting up the problem of the origin of religion in misery and that the world is full of misery and wickedness, Hume questions what kind of deity would one come to, given the existence of misery in the world. (See arguments against theism discussed earlier.) He discusses various answers and discounts each. He shows that no natural evil is necessary and that it is all avoidable. He allows that for all one knows that there might be an easy answer, but that this is unknown to man. At least this counts for some reason against belief in an all good, all powerful God.

Hume's argument can be accepted as far as it goes. No natural evil is necessary. The free will solution also allows that one could be free without the actuality or possibility, or necessity for evil. Theists generally show the possibility of compatibility between evil and the divine goodness. They do not show *why* there is evil. A theist could develop an answer by looking at the nature of good and evil in greater depth. Good for man as a rational being is the use of reason to the fullest. But reason is used to understand the nature of the world. And the nature of the world, for the theist, reveals the nature of the Creator. So, good for man is the knowledge of God. And evil is failing to have this knowledge. This assumes that it is clear that only some is eternal, that God the Creator exists—a position which has been argued for earlier. Evil in this view, serves the good by deepening the revelation of the divine nature. The divine justice and mercy are revealed by the presence of evil in a way that would not and could not be revealed otherwise.

Man is brought to knowledge of this deepened revelation in the course of history. Evil must be allowed to come to expression in all its forms and in every combination of admixture with the good. In the process, evil as unbelief is gradually removed, and the good as the knowledge of God is realized. This solution assumes the clarity of general revelation, that there is no other way to deepen the revelation, and that the knowledge of God is the good. The existence of evil cannot be justified by virtue or happiness, but by the good itself alone. By seeing the inexcusability of evil as a failure to see what is clear, the problem of evil is dissolved.[5] For moral evil not only serves the good, but one cannot object to the existence of evil when one is the source of it and when it is a voluntary closing of one's eyes to avoid seeing what is clear. And natural evil, since it is not necessary originally, is seen as imposed on man in order to bring man to stop and think, that is, to restrain, recall from, and remove moral evil.

Hume's second objection against religion based on miracles is adequate when an evidentialist approach is used to defend religious belief. For example, when belief in the resurrection is used to support belief in the deity of Christ and the truth of the Christian faith. The brute facts of the reports of the resurrection can be interpreted variously, at least in ways that do not rationally require belief. But instead of arguing from the actuality of the resurrection to belief in God, one should argue from belief in God to the necessity of the resurrection. The necessity for the resurrection is to be established before the actuality of it. As it is, Hume argues from the impossibility of the

---

5. Gangadean, *Philosophical Foundation*, 158-163.

resurrection to the non-occurrence of it. How can the necessity of the resurrection be shown?

If the existence of God can be shown from clear general revelation, then the existence of natural evil can be shown as not being original, given the infinite power and goodness of God. Natural evil is imposed subsequent to the creation and after the occurrence of moral evil. And natural evil—culminating in physical death—is imposed, not as punishment, since it is not inherent to moral evil. It is imposed as a call back from moral evil. And if physical death is imposed as a call back, then when moral evil is removed, natural evil will also be removed. The removal of physical death requires resurrection. The argument for the resurrection is based, therefore, on the existence and nature of natural evil. Furthermore, the occurrence of the resurrection of Christ is to be understood in the context of the requirement of redemption. Only when the requirement of the death of the redeemer is seen can the necessity of his resurrection be considered. Then it is not a matter of reasoning from the possibility of a miracle to the actuality of a miracle. Rather, we argue from the necessity for a miracle and from the consequences of the resurrection (overcoming moral and natural evil) to the actuality of the resurrection.

Chapter 16

———

KANT

BECAUSE MANY THEISTS HAVE NOT BEEN critical in their assumption of empiricism, they have been unable to head off Hume's criticisms, which are merely more consistent implications of empiricism that lead to skepticism. Hume's criticisms are valuable to awaken one from dogmatic slumber.

Immanuel Kant (1724–1804) attempted to respond to the shortcomings of rationalism and of empiricism. The thoughtfulness of his response is proportionate to the response given to his work by subsequent philosophers. He wanted to avoid the skepticism of Humean empiricism and the dogmatism of Leibnizian rationalism. He tried to show how both reason and sense experience combined to make human knowledge possible. Further, he wanted to show how both science and religion are possible and how neither obscures the possibility of morality, but how the freedom of morality is preserved from the encroachment of science, and how morality becomes the foundation for belief in God and the immortality of the soul when reason reaches its limits in regard to religion.

EPISTEMOLOGY:
Kant's Copernican Revolution

In contrast to empiricism, Kant argued that the mind is active in the process of knowing. It does not merely receive sensory input, but is active in ordering and shaping and relating this input. In addition to the effects of the forms of outer and inner intuition (space and time, respectively), the mind imposes on its sensible data the categories of the intellect, which include the notions of substance, unity, modality, and causality. Kant's explanation of the activity of the mind in knowing is likened to a Copernican revolution in philosophy. For ages, it was assumed that the mind was passive in knowing, even as it was thought the sun was active, but the earth was passive and motionless. Now everything has been changed, even reversed. The mind is active in shaping the world; it perceives by its concepts derived from the intellect itself. Mind and perception cooperate in knowledge formation as form and content. Percepts without concepts are blind, and concepts without percepts are empty.

In contrast to rationalism, Kant argued that knowledge of the world as it is in itself is not possible for man. We know the world as it appears to us, having been shaped by the activity of the mind. There have been interminable arguments in metaphysics regarding God, creation, and freedom because the limits of reason have not been observed. The certitude that we have is because the mind imposes itself in certain ways on all that appears to us. Time, space, and causality all belong to the world of phenomena, not to the noumenal world, the world as it is in itself. We have certitude about the world we see, in contrast to Hume's skepticism. But we do not have certitude about the world as it is in itself because the categories are from the mind and do not belong to the world in itself. In addition to *a posteriori* judgments (about things we experience, but do not have certainty about) and in addition to *a priori* judgments (which are necessary truths of reason, but not about the world), there are *synthetic a priori* judgments which are both certain and give knowledge of the world as it is experienced.

To say that we can say nothing about the noumenal world and yet say that there is such a world, with a one-to-one correspondence between things in the noumenal world and the phenomenal world, is contradictory, on the face of it. Furthermore, to say that causality does not apply to the noumenal world is, on the face of it, unwarranted. First, because if we can say nothing about that world, positively or negatively, then to say causality does not apply to it is to say too much. Just because causality is in the mind does not make it necessarily true that it is not also in the world. The same can be said of reason, which can be both the laws of thought and the laws of being.

Second, Kant implies that there is at least a causal connection between the noumenal world and the phenomenal world in that noumenal being is the cause of what we encounter in the phenomenal world. The cause of what I see could possibly be another mind, as Berkeley suggested. But Kant speaks of specific objects in that world corresponding to objects in this world, such as a chair-in-itself. Since the noumenal world is a cause of what I see, causality cannot be excluded from the noumenal world. Also, since the changes in this world correspond to changes in the noumenal world, one would assume that in the noumenal world, changes are caused. The alternative is to say that the noumenal world is not subject to change, that it is an atemporal world, but this leaves the cause of change in this world unexplained. Kant was not willing to slip into the idealism of Berkeley to avoid this problem. Later philosophers such as Hegel and Schopenhauer were willing to offer an idealist explanation of the working of the noumenal world.

CAUSALITY AND FREEDOM

Two motives operate to push Kant into his view of the noumenal world. First, there are the antinomies of pure reason (for example, the world has a beginning in time and the world has no beginning in time), which can be avoided, in Kant's view, by claiming that reason is reaching beyond its limits and naturally falls into such quandaries. Such a drastic step need not be taken. There is yet room for reason to operate critically by examining assumptions in the way the problem is stated. Second, by restricting causality to the phenomenal world, Kant believed he simultaneously provided for the world of science in which causality and determinism reign and in which there is no freedom, and the world of morality, in the noumenal realm, which is free from the demands of causality. This solution leaves me determined and not free in the phenomenal world while I am at the same time free in the noumenal world. Since my consciousness of myself is unitary and not split into two views of myself, how am I to regard myself—as both free and not free, at the same time and in the same respect? And how am I to be regarded and treated by others? Am I responsible for the theft in the noumenal world, but not responsible in the phenomenal world? Am I punished in the one world, but not in the other? Kant's solution of two worlds or two views of one world raises more questions than it settles.

Kant need not have gone in this direction to resolve the problem of freedom. Other solutions are possible and more plausible. Kant assumes that causality is incompatible with freedom. *Ought* implies *can*, and *can* is incompatible with causality. Given the cause, the effect necessarily follows. In Kant's view, if my act is caused, then I could not do otherwise. He considers any attempt to avoid the implication that *ought* implies *can* to be a wretched subterfuge. He thereby rejects the position of soft determinists who maintain that causality and freedom are compatible. I am caused, yet I am free if the cause is from within me and not merely external. My wants may be caused by what I believe, and given my wants, I may not be able to do otherwise, yet since I am pursuing my wants, I am free.

Freedom is doing what I want, not the freedom to do otherwise. God is free, yet being infinitely and eternally good, cannot do evil. There is no gap between *want* and *can* at the basic level. If I wanted to, I could have done otherwise. If I wanted to, I could and now can use my reason critically in order to know what is clear. I am, therefore, always responsible for my beliefs and the wants which flow from these beliefs. So, even if my wants are caused, they are caused by me, that is, from my beliefs and that from my willingness to use reason. No one can say: "I want to use my reason, but I can't." Kant, therefore, did not have to try to gain freedom by excluding causality from the world as it is in itself.

DEONTOLOGICAL ETHICS

In showing what we are morally obligated to do, Kant argues first of all for the ultimate worth of a will that is moved by reason alone without any regard for personal happiness. "Nothing can possibly be conceived in the world, or even out of it, which can be called good, without qualification, except a good will."[1] In fact, he says, "a good will appears to constitute the indispensable condition even of being worthy of happiness."[2] Kant thus sets his moral position squarely against utilitarians who make happiness the *summum bonum* and the goal of all morality. Thus, Kant seems to be the philosopher who exalts the claims of reason above all else so that when deficiencies appear

---

1. Immanuel Kant, *Fundamental Principles of the Metaphysic of Morals* (New York: Bobbs-Merrill Company, Inc., 1949), 11.

2. Kant, *Fundamental Principles of the Metaphysic of Morals*, 11.

in his position, they are considered the deficiencies of reason rather than Kant's deficiency in the use of reason. Reason dictates the duty of a rational man. And a rational man will pursue duty for duty's sake and not for the sake of happiness. Kant's position is a paradigm case of deontology. Is deontology able to withstand rational scrutiny?

What are the deliverances of reason in regard to moral obligation? Kant distinguishes the hypothetical from the categorical imperative or command of reason. A hypothetical imperative commands thus: if you want x, you must do y. The categorical imperative has no regard for my wants and commands me without qualification: "act only on those maxims which can be willed to be universal laws."[3] Thus universalizability is the clear indication of rationality, since reason is equally binding on all men. Criticisms have been raised by showing that there can be a conflict of duties in what reason commands. To keep a promise may conflict with saving an innocent human life, both of which are regarded as maxims required by the categorical imperative. To escape this conflict, I may qualify one of these commands. But to do so can trivialize the universalizability thesis. Furthermore, strange things may be universalized at times.

All of these difficulties arise from Kant's deontology, which regards virtue as the end in itself rather than the means to the end. The natural limits and source of unity are missing in considering virtue apart from the good. Therefore, the maxims can conflict when unqualified, become overqualified without the guidance of the good, and can allow strange things to be universalized when the good is not in place. Kant fails to see that the good must be based on our view of human nature, which in turn is based on our view of what is real. Kant's metaphysics disallows any knowledge of what is real because the noumenal world is beyond the limits of human knowledge. Kant reverses this order and derives the existence of God and the immortality of the soul as necessary conditions for morality. Kant does not see the inherent connection between the good and happiness. And since the virtues are regarded independently of the good rather than as a means to the good, neither is there any natural connection between virtue and happiness. The possibility of a virtuous person being in an unending state of misery was an unsatisfactory state of affairs, even though happiness was

---

3. Kant, *Fundamental Principles of the Metaphysic of Morals*, 19.

not to be the motive or the reward for virtue in Kant's metaphysics of morals. The only way to guarantee any connection between virtue and happiness was through the agency of one who had the power to bring this connection about. And the only one who could do so was God. Kant postulated God as a necessary condition for morality to make this connection. But in doing so, Kant calls into question the original purity of the good will (a will moved by reason without regard for happiness), which was of the highest possible value for him. And because happiness is extrinsic to virtue, it is not the happiness of the rational man by virtue of being rational (that is, it is not the happiness that comes from the knowledge of God), but one more connected with his sensible or bodily nature, thereby further debasing the dignity of man, which Kant set out to uphold.

Kant does not argue from the necessity of immortality to rationally justify moral effort, but derives the necessity of immortality from the time needed to achieve the goal of moral perfection. The difficulty of achieving a good will is so great that no one can hope to achieve it in this lifetime. And since *ought* implies *can*, and *ought* is certainly given in man's moral consciousness, for Kant, there must, of necessity, be immortality for the goal to be achieved. But mere duration is not enough. Some may loiter forever in the shallow waters of morality and not ever get there. And if the goal is to get there and some do achieve a good will, then there is no further need for continued existence. Upon achieving the goal, one may thereby guarantee one's own extinction. Either some will not get there, and so immortality is of no avail, or some will eventually get there, in which case immortality is of no further use. In either case, Kant does not succeed in justifying belief in immortality for the sake of achieving the good will. The argument from mere continued progression to perfection while never reaching it and that progress being regarded by God as equivalent to achieving perfection is not sufficient to require immortality for morality. If mere progress is sufficient, in place of achieving it, then it becomes arbitrary at what point progress is considered sufficient for morality.

Having blocked any possible knowledge of God by his epistemological dualism of the phenomenal and the noumenal world, Kant proceeds to interpret religious belief in terms of the rational requirements of ethical theory. He ventures far into the realm of traditional Christian terminology and gives what he believes is the content of a rational man's faith. He does so in the spirit of the Enlightenment, whose motto is: *sapere aude!*—Have the courage to use your own understanding. The goal of the Enlightenment is man's freedom, his emergence from his self-incurred immaturity, through the use of his own reason. What cannot be derived from reason cannot be binding.

Since religion and scriptures make claims not derivable from reason, Kant attempts to systematically reinterpret good and evil, the fallen condition of man, and the coming of the kingdom of God in terms consistent with his ethical theory. The beginning of his reinterpretation is his understanding of freedom. He distinguishes the function of the will into two parts, the *wille*, which gives the moral law as the command of reason to the will, and the *willkur*, which determines the weight of the motives which move the will and which acts on the weightiest motive as freely determined by the *willkur*. Here the question must be asked how the motives are weighed. Is it a rational process at all, and if so, how can a lesser motive rationally receive greater weight than the greater motive? If the motives have no weight in themselves, but are assigned weight by *willkur*, how can this be rational or irrational, and how can any blame be attached to either choice of assignment of weight? What Kant had in mind appears to be the wrong of putting considerations of our sensible nature above our rational nature. Evil is understood in dualist terms as resulting from a conflict between the rational and the non-rational aspects of our being.

What is noteworthy here is Kant's concept of good and evil, the assumption regarding human nature, and the origin of human nature, which are all the classical pieces necessary for an adequate ethical theory. Evil is not the failure to use reason to see what is clear, a failure arising in the soul and not from the body; evil is less serious than that for Kant. "Man is evil can only mean, He is conscious of the moral law but has nevertheless adopted into his maxims the (occasional) deviation there from."[4] Evil is not radical, affecting his whole being; it is occasional. Man is not spiritually dead regarding seeking God and understanding clear general revelation, requiring God's act to be restored to life in order to see what is clear. He needs help only after man makes himself worthy of God's assistance. "Where shall we start,

---

4. Immanuel Kant, *Basic Writings of Kant* (New York: The Modern library, 2001), 382.

i.e., with a faith in what God has done on our behalf, or with what we are to do to become worthy of God's assistance (whatever this may be)? In answering this question, we cannot hesitate in deciding for the second alternative."[5] A superficial view of evil can only require a superficial need for grace.

Like many before, claiming to be champions of reason, Kant denies the necessity for special revelation. Ecclesiastical faith is grounded in special revelation. This must give way to the demands of reason in due time. This is the coming of the kingdom of God. He says, "The gradual transition of ecclesiastical faith to the exclusive sovereignty of pure religious faith is the coming of the kingdom of God."[6] What is particularly difficult to see is that the requirements of reason for special revelation are denied in the name of reason. Those sent by God are often killed in the name of God. If the self-appointed champions of reason do these things in the name of reason, what shall others do? Kant responded to the antinomy of empiricism and rationalism by a synthesis of both, continuing to hold their assumptions, and managed to account for knowledge by an unwarranted restriction of knowledge to the world of appearance. This is not an acceptable solution to the problem of skepticism.

---

5. Immanuel Kant, *Religion within the Bounds of Bare Reason* (Indianapolis: Hackitt Publishing Company, 2009), 131.

6. Kant, *Religion within the Bounds of Bare Reason*, 115.

Chapter 17

HEGEL

G EORG WILHELM FRIEDRICH HEGEL'S (1770–1831) grand philosophy rests on his understanding of the nature of being and
non-being and the relation of these two in the process of change. All
of reality is of one kind. "Nowhere in heaven or on earth is there anything which does not contain within itself both being and nothing."[1]
This includes God. In fact, God is just the sum total of all that is for
Hegel. God undergoes change. God develops through history. "History in general is . . . the development of Spirit in time . . . ."[2]

THE NATURE OF BEING,
NON-BEING, AND BECOMING

Being, for Hegel, is the indeterminate. "It is free from determinate-
ness in relation to essence ... This reflectionless being is being as it is
immediately in its own self alone."[3] But nothing is also indeterminate.
"Nothing is, therefore, the same determination, or rather absence of
determination, and thus altogether the same as, pure being."[4] These
unusual definitions of "being" and "nothing" carry into all of Hegel's thoughts and bring about that all of his terms have an unusual
meaning. Many of the usual questions cannot be asked of Hegel's

---

1. Georg Wilhelm Friedrich Hegel, *The Science of Logic* (Cambridge: Cambridge University Press, 2015), 61.
2. Georg Wilhelm Friedrich Hegel, *Philosophy of History*, *Great Books of the Western World, Vol. 43*. (Chicago: Encyclopedia Britannica, 1994), 185.
3. Hegel, *The Science of Logic*, 59.
4. Hegel, *The Science of Logic*, 59.

metaphysics without having an uncomfortable feeling of them being somewhat forced, given his unusual starting point.

Perhaps the issue lies in his conception of reason or of reasoning. Hegel makes much of reason as he understands it. Reason is not so much the laws of thought or the laws of being in general, but reason is the law of change. Since there is nothing that is not an intermediate between being and nothing, these two are always in relation, in Hegel's view, and must be regarded so. He says of reasoning, which separates the two:

> This style of reasoning which makes and clings to the false presupposition of the absolute separateness of being and non-being is to be named not dialectic but sophistry. For sophistry is an argument proceeding from a baseless presupposition which is uncritically and unthinkingly adopted; but we call the dialectic the higher movement of reason in which such seemingly utterly separate terms pass over into each other spontaneously, through that which they are, a movement in which the presupposition sublates itself.[5]

Since it is unclear how non-being is different from being and how, therefore, two things that are non-different can be combined to produce a third higher being, we can try various possible interpretations of Hegel's view. How does being "pass over" into non-being and vice versa? Does being become non-being, and does non-being become being? Is non-being a potentiality of being which it comes to actualize? Does non-being combine with being? Or, is non-being just a way of speaking about what is the other to a being, such as *a* and *non-a*, white and non-white? Is Hegel speaking of the indeterminate (being) becoming determinate (non-being)? These questions at least draw attention to the need to clarify the meaning of basic terms in Hegel. The issue may not be resolvable at this level, but neither should it go unnoticed in any future reflections on Hegel.

There is an instance that may help clarify what Hegel means. He regards Christianity as the highest form of positive religion because of its teaching regarding the Incarnation. In the Incarnation, "the infinite is not distinct from what is finite, but is necessarily manifest in

---

5. Hegel, *The Science of Logic*, 90.

it."[6] In the creed of Chalcedon, the Incarnation is understood as the divine taking to itself human nature. This was later further explained in the Westminster Confession (1648), "So that two whole, perfect, and distinct natures, the Godhead and the manhood, were inseparably joined together in one person, without conversion, composition, or confusion."[7] Here, the infinite does not become finite, as Hegel suggests. The infinite and the finite are distinct and remain so.

If the infinite could become finite and vice versa, then there is nothing unusual going on in the Incarnation, since it would be going on everywhere, always. In fact, one would not be able to distinguish the two, even as non-being cannot be distinguished from being. And if distinctions cannot be made, then change or development cannot be said to occur. If spirit is not distinct from matter, then it is not the case that *non-a* changes or "passes over" to become *a*. Change presupposes permanence and distinctness of essences. But a change within a form is not a change into another form.

HISTORY AND THE ACTUALIZATION OF SPIRIT

Other equally puzzling or contradictory states of affairs arise in Hegel's view. He regards the history of change as the Spirit actualizing its potential from a lesser to a greater fullness. Perhaps this can be restated to mean matter is realizing its potential to become spirit or non-matter. The concept of potential within a form becomes the potential to become another or any form in Hegel. It would follow from this formulation of potentiality that *a* is potentially *non-a*, and *non-a* is potentially *a*. So that spirit is potentially matter as well as matter is potentially spirit. It is not that both spirit and matter exist and by uniting the two become a more complex being. That would not be consistent with going from a less conscious to a more conscious being, although even here, the conscious is in the unconscious even as the unconscious is in the conscious. There is nothing which is distinct in Hegel; all collapses into one state of flux. It is like trying to find a black cow on a black night.

---

6. Hegel, *The Science of Logic*, 138.

7. *Westminster Confession of Faith*, 8.2, Of Christ the Mediator.

How a being can actualize itself without the aid of another remains a mystery. In Aristotle, what becomes actual is actualized by another. He found the source of all change in an unchanging being, a Prime Mover. Materialists who affirm an eternal process nevertheless see the process as remaining material from beginning to end. There is no actualization, just change, in an endless cycle. Hegel's view of Spirit actualizing itself is a form of self-creation and encounters all the self-contradiction inherent in that notion. Gradual self-creation, in stages, is still self-creation. At every point, one would have to exist before one existed in order to bring oneself into existence. But if Hegel can unite being and non-being to produce a higher order of being, the contradiction of self-creation would not be any greater hurdle for him.

There is yet another critical point in Hegel that seems not to fit with other things in his system. He speaks of the goal of history as if there eventually comes an end to the dialectical process. The goal of history is freedom as self-consciousness. The state is the end of history, the embodiment of Reason. "Truth is the unity of the universe and the subjective will; and the universal is to be found in the State, in its laws . . . ."[8] Self-consciousness came to full expression in the Prussian state of Hegel's day and in the philosophy of Hegel. History moves to its end by movements through periods, and we are led to this culmination by the motive power of will, which is especially embodied in world-historical heroes. Napoleon embodied that will in his day. There is not only the problem of explaining why the dialectic will not go on and perhaps go on endlessly, if it does not lapse into a repeating cycle, and the problem of why the end was not already reached (assuming it can be reached) given an infinite past time, but there is a sort of quaintness in thinking the fullness of history was reached in his day, in his State, and in his philosophy. A measure of egocentrism is pardonable in all men, but this, as the highest achievement of Spirit, falls short of the longing of mankind for the ideal. Perhaps it is inevitable when there is no conception of a transcendent being beyond the historical process that the latest phase of history is naturally the very best that there is. Still, the dairymaid and the cobbler long for more. Hegel's god is too small.

---

8. Hegel, *Philosophy of History*, 178.

Chapter 18

___

EXISTENTIALISM

KIERKEGAARD

SOREN KIERKEGAARD (1813–1855) BECAME THE founder of existentialism by focusing on the individual having to act decisively in a concrete situation, which decision, he believed could not be guided by reason. Reason grasps the universal, not the particular. Kierkegaard reacted to Hegel's absorption of the individual into a mere moment in the expression of the life of the Absolute. He reacted also to the sterility of the Church in his day as failing to grasp the depth and grandeur of the life of faith. In *Fear and Trembling*, he attempted to show that faith goes beyond reason (he called it the teleological suspension of the ethical) by describing how Abraham became the knight of faith and the father of the faithful in his act of offering up his son Isaac as a burnt offering, in obedience to God's command.

His passionate and literary (at times, lyrical) style persuaded many to adopt his view of faith as a leap, going beyond reason. For Kierkegaard faith not only goes beyond reason, but against it. The faithful must believe "by reason of the absurd" that he must act contrary to reason and the universal law of God which forbids murder. And though he gives up to death by sacrificing his son Isaac whom he loves above all else, yet he will receive Isaac back from the dead, in order that the promises of God may be fulfilled through Isaac, and not through anyone else.

Is this so? Is faith a leap that goes beyond or against reason? Is going beyond reason necessary to realize fully one's unique individuality? I think not. Rather, faith is reason operating in its fullest degree. Faith is not opposed to reason, but to the senses. While the senses give us the visible, faith through reason grasps the invisible. Faith grows as understanding grows, and faith is tested as the understanding is tested.

Kierkegaard's analysis of the story of Abraham does not recognize sufficiently the concrete situation in which Abraham acted. Contrary to the intention of existentialism, it abstracts Abraham's decision from the concrete situation in which he acted. To see if Abraham's offering up of his son Isaac went beyond reason, Abraham's set of beliefs and reasons for these beliefs must be considered. His decision to offer up Isaac is not to be isolated from what went earlier in his life, from decisions he made earlier, and from the reason for these decisions.

A reader of the story of Abraham must consider several crucial moments in Abraham's life.

1. Abraham's decision to leave Ur of the Chaldees reflected his belief in the existence of God as Creator and ruler of mankind, his view of good and evil past, and his view of the future outcome of the conflict of good and evil. Ur was not a city of God, and it was doomed to destruction because of this. Its unbelief was inexcusable. The blessing will come on all mankind through the offspring promised to Abraham. To inherit the promised land is something that will occur far beyond his lifetime. The promised land is here on earth; it is not heaven. If the promised land is to be inherited by Abraham, he would have to be raised from the dead to receive the promise. He must have seen death as a consequence of moral evil, not part of the original creation, that death was imposed as part of the curse that will be removed when moral evil is removed from the earth. The promised great nation would be the center of a culture that lives in obedience to God's word. All nations would come to live in obedience to God's command in order that all nations might receive God's blessing. Abraham's world and life view enabled him to leave all worldly comfort and security to go to a promised land where his life would be constantly threatened. This decision required so much of him that it must have required deep reflection on and commitment to everything he understood of good and evil

2. Abraham knew the significance of sacrifice for sin. It showed his recognition of the reality of sin and the necessity of the death of another to pay for his sin. When asked to offer up Isaac as a sacrifice he

must have understood the difference between sacrifice and mere killing or murder. He knew the need for the innocent to die in the place of the guilty, and he also knew that animal sacrifice was not sufficient to pay the penalty, but was typifying what was sufficient but was yet to be more fully revealed and yet to come.

3. Abraham knew the significance of circumcision. Circumcision was a sign of the need for a new heart. Applied to infants, it meant that infants, too, had the reality of sin and had the need for a new heart, a spiritual rebirth from spiritual death.

4. Abraham knew the power of God to bring life out of death. He had waited long for an offspring. He had thought Lot would be his offspring by adoption, since Sarah, his wife, had been so far barren. He thought Eleazar, his steward, might be the one in his household through whom the promise would be fulfilled. He thought the child he had through Hagar, by Sarah's advice, would be his promised child. Finally, when he was one hundred years old, and Sarah was ninety and her womb was dead, she conceived and gave birth to Isaac, as God had earlier promised. As he called the child each day by his name Isaac, he was reminded that with God, all things were possible. He saw each day before him how life was brought out of death by God, in order to fulfill the promise. Man is utterly dependent on God to receive the promise of life.

5. It is in this concrete situation that Abraham receives the command of God to sacrifice Isaac. He had heard the voice of God many times before. He knew that as a prophet, God revealed to him what God would do. As he goes to sacrifice Isaac, he believes they will both return again, that God himself will provide the sacrifice, that God would fulfill his promise, even if God had to raise Isaac from the dead to fulfill the promise through Isaac. He knew that Isaac, whom he had circumcised, had sin and could not be the sacrifice for sin. He had believed in the resurrection of the dead before he left Ur; it was reinforced by the miraculous manner of Isaac's birth. He reasoned that God would raise Isaac from the dead to fulfill the promise.

6. The promise had to do with the removal of moral evil (sin) from the world, and this was to be done through the sacrifice, and yet Isaac could not be that sacrifice, but one who was to come through Isaac, one whom God himself would provide. It was in this context that Abraham came to realize the significance of what he was doing in the sacrifice of his son, his only son Isaac, whom he loved. He saw he was called to do what God himself would one day do for the removal of the sin of the world, including his own and Isaac's. He saw that day and was glad. In knowing what it is for the father to offer up his only son, he came to be called the friend of God.

This understanding of his act of offering up Isaac was not contrary to reason, but a necessary development of all else he had understood about the nature of God and of good and evil. By observing the details of Abraham's life in its concrete particulars, it can be seen that faith is not contrary to reason, but requires the fullest development of the use of reason to understand the human condition in general and one's own condition in particular.

NIETZSCHE

Friedrich Nietzsche (1844–1900), speaking through Zarathustra, declared, God is dead. Speaking more literally, he means that God is not any longer relevant in the thinking of modern man. He means further that those who hold to belief in God restrict their lives in ways that are harmful to themselves and others. Man is restricted from being all that he can be, from being the superman. The morality of Christianity, to love your neighbor as yourself, is a slave morality, not fitted for the superman, who may achieve his transcendence by subjugating the interests of others to himself. Slave morality is for the masses, which wants none to excel above others. This is inimical to the drive to be superhuman, an essential quality of life conceived in evolutionary terms. Further, Christianity is seen as encouraging other-worldliness and despising the life of the body. It is suspicious of strong emotions and strong thinking; it is neither Dionysian nor Apollonian, the poles between which the superman lives. In short, Nietzsche said, God is dead.

A wit has replied: God said, Nietzsche is dead, that is, spiritually dead. Or Nietzsche's God is dead. Or it is the twilight for the God with whom Nietzsche was acquainted. It appears that the Christianity Nietzsche inveighs against is the Christianity of popular culture, reinforced by tradition. And in much of what he says, he is correct. But what he says is directed against a strawman and reflects the same lack of thinking he objects to in popular religion. He could have argued as Kierkegaard did against popular religion by proposing a deeper, more thoughtful form of Christianity. But his antipathy from personal experience hindered him. At some point, he abandoned belief in God for the prevailing naturalistic interpretation of origins and developed the implications of evolution for life in the doctrine of the superman.

Marx, Nietzsche, and Freud all accepted and built upon the teachings of Darwin. They all viewed belief in the supernatural world as contrary to science and a hindrance to man's full development. Most of their objections apply in some measure to popular forms of Christianity. However, the central core of their objection is against the existence of God in the name of science. The critical objection to their position is to show first that it is clear that God exists, second, that the naturalistic interpretation of the origin of human life and the cosmos is inadequate and begs the question, and that the form of theism being objected to is the popular and not the historic or philosophical form of theism.

SARTRE

Jean-Paul Sartre (1905–1980) adopts the atheistic view of existentialism. Specifically, he believes man does not have a preexisting nature in light of which he must act. Man's existence precedes his essence. Man becomes what he is by his choice. Man cannot escape choosing. He is necessarily free. He is authentically free when he accepts full responsibility for his choice.

Man cannot plead any extenuating circumstance which requires him to choose as he does. If a person does not cooperate with the underground resistance to the Nazis occupying France during WWII, it is his own choice. Being an only son of an ailing mother cannot excuse his choice not to join. Man gives meaning to all relations. They have no meaning in themselves. Since there is no God who determines meaning, man must necessarily be in the place of God to determine the meaning of things. The existence or non-existence of God is not a matter of indifference. It makes all the difference in the world. Without God, man is left to his own resources. He is alone and forlorn in his freedom. Reason is of no use for there are no essences to be grasped by reason which can then guide man in his freedom.

Sartre gives a story that illustrates man's condition. Suppose one is driving along on a rainy day and sees someone walking along in the rain. The driver can choose freely between three alternatives. He may stop and give a ride to the person walking along. He may drive on by. Or he may run over the pedestrian. One choice is not to be preferred over another by reason. If the life of the person is spared because it is valued, then the value of life is not there objectively, but because one chooses to give it value. There is no essence in things that is the source of value. The value is bestowed by a free choice independent of any demand of reason. Value is freely bestowed, and the recognition of that free bestowal is authentic freedom.

How does Sartre come to this position? Does he justify his atheism? Does he justify his view that there are no essences or that there can be no essences? Is it possible to bestow essence by choice? Is meaning the same as essence, so that to bestow the former is to bestow the latter? And is authentic freedom possible? Are choices undirected by any possible consideration of reason possible? Did or could Sartre act consistently with his teaching?

It appears at times that Sartre's existentialism is an inference from atheism. At times, it appears that universal change governs all being and that, therefore, there can be no essences or fixed natures for any being. The Heraclitan view of flux or the contemporary view of change in evolution is assumed in Sartre. At times atheism is assumed as obvious; at times it is assumed as the reasonable alternative if skepticism is true. The focus of his attention is not metaphysical or epistemological, but ethical: the act of the will consciously asserting itself is what commands attention. The individual without the guidance of reason asserts his existence by choosing in a concrete situation.

Sartre's ontology has to reckon with the question of whether reason is ontological, applying to being as well as thought, as well as whether reason is transcendental. Without this, all speech is empty and without meaning and it is impossible even to choose to give meaning. Reason is a test of meaning. To deny the applicability of reason is to deny the possibility of meaning. But if reason is ontological, then we can know that there must be something eternal and that only some is eternal. And Sartre's view of man being alone, without God, and without any possible guidance from reason would not have application.

Although Sartre argues for authentic freedom, he does not allow all choices to be equal. He wishes others to choose not to collaborate with the Nazis. He wishes others to join the cause of freedom for the Algerians. If he were consistent, the alternative choice would do just as well. His failure to grant equality to alternative choice is an indication of bad faith, something he exhorts all persons to avoid. Perhaps it cannot be avoided, since we cannot be in the place of God to determine the meaning of things, to determine good and evil for ourselves. To retain meaning without reason is impossible. Being, without reason, is nothingness.

CAMUS

Albert Camus (1913–1960) begins his work on *the Myth of Sisyphus* with the most basic philosophical question for him, that of suicide. Man is confronted with a decision that cannot be made on the basis of reason—whether life is or is not worth living. The context of life in which man must make his decision is that of the Absurd. Life is absurd because inescapably juxtaposed are man's need for the Absolute and the absence of the Absolute. No finite thing can satisfy man's longing for the Absolute. Sisyphus pushes the rock of melancholy out of his heart. As long as man is alive, he must seek happiness, he must push the rock. But without the Absolute, the rock he pushes inevitably rolls back down the hill. Can Sisyphus hope that he can roll the rock up the hill, never to roll back down again? Can man hope for happiness without the Absolute?

In light of the history of mankind and in light of one's own life, is there reason to hope? Not everyone faces the question of suicide. For some, the absurdity of life does not present itself. For these persons, their consciousness is not yet awakened. The multitude live a semi-conscious existence. For some, the question arises in the most mundane of activities and life becomes an incomprehensible dumb show in the face of which man experiences nausea. For this person what are the choices? First, there is ordinary suicide. Life is without meaning. End it. Then there is intellectual suicide. In God, life has meaning. But for Camus, to get to God one must abandon reason, for there is no reason to believe in God. Or lastly, one may face the absurdity of life and choose to live life although it is absurd, without mitigating its absurdity. One must push the rock by reason of the absurd, devoting every effort to accomplish what cannot be accomplished, or what has no worth even if it is accomplished.

Camus thinks that few can become the hero of the absurd. In several of his stories, he shows what it is like to live absurdly. In *The Plague*, the doctor strives valiantly against the plague, though it is hopeless. But this is a form of hopelessness we can yet understand, virtue apart from consequential considerations. Perhaps the more absurd condition is where it is equally as hopeless if all are saved from the plague. Camus does not consider this possibility. He is still the inheritor of meaning from a Biblical tradition of virtue. He has no philosophical warrant to import the notion of virtue into his account of life without committing philosophical suicide. He has mitigated the absurd.

Perhaps no man can truly live with the absurd. True absurdity is death, and one cannot be in death and be alive. Music and random noise are not alike. A Rembrandt and a decomposing rat are not equally to be viewed. A story of philosophical significance and nursery rhymes are not equally meaningful. Camus consistently chose to write philosophically. His writing itself is the objection to his view of the absurd.

Chapter 19

———

MODERNITY AND
POSTMODERNITY

AN INTRODUCTION

THE MODERN PERIOD OF PHILOSOPHY (1650–1950) began with
challenges to the medieval worldview by means of experiences
overseas and exploring new geography; breakthroughs in the sciences
and astronomy; and innovations such as the printing press. There were
new lands, peoples, cultures, and civilizations to consider. The Renais-
sance returned to classical (Hellenistic) culture. The Reformation returned to the historic Christian faith in response to challenges. With
the Reformation came the disunity of Christendom. Religious wars
following the Reformation led to the Peace of Westphalia in 1648.

The Enlightenment highlighted the antinomies of Rationalism
and empiricism in epistemology and drifted towards Deism in metaphysics in a move to distance philosophy from theism. Deism opened
the door further to naturalism, from Newton (the cosmos) to Darwin
(the evolution of life forms). Natural law extended to all. There is no
creation and no providence. Naturalism led to secularism—a focus on
this world—and to the growth of atheistic worldviews such as Marx's
Utopianism.

Modernity came with revolution and the overthrow of the remnants of monarchy, aristocracy, and feudalism, in favor of *lex rex* and
constitutionalism (liberty, equality, fraternity). Modernity closed with
the fall of empires, the end of colonialism, and the two world wars.
The post-flood world saw the rise and fall of the empires of Egypt,
Hittite, Babylon, Assyria, and Persia; The ancient world saw the rise
and fall of the empires of Greece, Rome, India, and China; and the

modern world saw the rise and fall of the Spanish, French, German, British, Japanese, and Hungarian empires.

The post-modern period of philosophy (1950–2000s) began with the challenges of the Cold War and China's proxy wars, and with this liberal individualism vs. socialist collectivism, where the whole of society is the real, and the individual (parts) serves the whole. The whole serves its rulers (individuals) cynically with a trace of irony. Postmodernity arrives with post-colonialism, pluralism, and the rise of multiculturalism.

The post-World War II years brought an unraveling with the deaths of John F. Kennedy and Martin Luther King, the war in Vietnam, and East-West relations. The Baby Boomer generation created a counter-culture around sex, drugs, and rock and roll. Second (1960s–1980s) and Third wave feminism (1990s–2000s) became ever more radical. Critical Theory (1930s–2000s) and Postmodernism (1940s–2000s) provided the means of deconstructing the remnants of the Modern period. Neo-Marxist critical theorists developed a critique of Western culture first based on economic, then cultural oppression where the minority group is oppressed by the majority, and there is unseen systemic racism (Critical Race Theory).

The postmodern age is marked by culture wars and identity politics. Postmodern thinking is laden with skepticism, idealism (vs. realism), ethical relativism, politically correct language, and subjectivism. Once again, man is the measure of all thought. The latter part of the postmodern era is facing the prospect of the conflict between globalism and a one-world government (New World Order) or a return to nationalism (nation, kindred, tribe, and tongue). This is a conflict from Babel.

There is a spiritual war between belief and unbelief, which is age-long and agonizing, and good will overcome evil. History, in the form of challenge and response, is the outworking of the spiritual war. This war is asymmetrical. One side fights with reason and truth (belief), and the other side with ideology and force. Falsehood may only be overcome with truth.

Chapter 20

———

DERRIDA ON DECONSTRUCTION

JACQUES DERRIDA (1930–2004) ACCEPTED THE assumption of Martin Heidegger (1889–1976) that "transcendental" questions were meaningless. Traditional metaphysical questions, after Kant, were thought to be no longer possible. Kantian assumptions were uncritically accepted, leading to skepticism. Along with this skepticism, the role of philosophy—past and future—was redefined. Philosophy was nothing other than the ideology of Western ethos. Its preeminence, as with all ideology, was its truth. To replace one ideology with another is to fall into a trap. Since we are always situated in history and from history, there was no transcendence, the only recourse in philosophy, which claims to hold reason absolute, was to use reason to expose the inherent contradictions in apparently reasonable positions. He called this strategy deconstruction.

Is it possible to escape being trapped by one's situatedness in the world? To be fallen is to interpret the ordinariness of life in terms of the tradition built upon the world one inherits. To escape this ordinariness, one must contemplate the end of ordinariness, that is, one's own death or non-being or nothingness. To achieve authenticity one must question authority, which includes questioning the meaning of words by breaking a word into its component parts in order to trace its history. The stratagem of deconstruction resists the power of reason in the name of history. In our situatedness in the world, the word or sign precedes the referent, according to Derrida. The creature dog is only recognizable as that after the sign "dog" has been applied to it. Consciousness never precedes language, and the meaning of language is known by an inquiry into writing. Every sign is a signifier whose signifier is another signifier. Thus, meaning is always deferred.

What is of interest here is the twofold claim that we are always situated, and that consciousness never precedes language. These are two universal claims, neither of which is self-evident or directly known to the senses. But the content of these claims disallows for any universal claims, since situatedness and language differ endlessly in time. The strategy of using empirical-historical claims to defeat the claims of reason, or to resist the claims of reason, so as not to be trapped by an ideology, seems to seek a transcendence which is confessed to be impossible. Reason is being used to defeat reason. This seems more of a hopeless trap than escaping situatedness. If there is any authenticity in the process, some truth claim is being made. And if so, there is an absoluteness about any truth claim, which sets it over against the falsehood of its opposite. No situatedness can overcome an authentic truth claim. And before language could be learned, the capacity to learn, requiring an *a priori* understanding of the difference between true and false must also be in place. There is no escape from the demands of reason.

Chapter 21

PLANTINGA

ALVIN PLANTINGA (1932–) IS A CONTEMPORARY philosopher who continues the tradition of reformed epistemology, with inimitable style. He traces his epistemological lineage from Plato, through Augustine, and Calvin. He holds an unofficial position of dean of Christian philosophers in the Society of Christian Philosophers. His contribution is to make clearer the implications of reformed epistemology, in light of recent and current challenges. Specifically, he addresses the question of rationality of belief in God in light of the foundationalist challenge. Does he show that belief in God is rational? And what, by implication or directly, does he say about the question of clarity of general revelation.

Plantinga has argued that the believer is within her epistemological right to believe in God without having to give a reason for such a belief. He does this by first addressing the question of how we define "know." Instead of starting with a definition of knowledge and seeing how particular examples measure up, he believes we must start with examples of knowing and derive the definition from these cases. Examples of knowledge would include that there is an external world, memory beliefs, and the existence of other minds. These beliefs are properly basic because they are not believed on the basis of any other beliefs. He then argues that belief in God is among beliefs which are properly basic for the believer, because it is typically not believed on the basis of any other beliefs, just as in the case of belief in the external world.

One may question whether belief in the external world is properly basic. Perhaps Plantinga means that if the antitheist accepts some beliefs without having a basis, then other beliefs may be worthy candidates for inclusion too. But this is merely a form of *tu quoque*, and has more sociological than philosophical interest. It does not address the criterion of properly basic. Properly basic for me, or for a group, or at this time, is not the same as logically basic. This question is raised all the more when we consider the notion of a defeater of a properly basic belief. The problem of evil is an apparent defeater of belief in God. There can be objections to these types of basic beliefs. And the believer is no longer within her rights to hold that belief until there is a defeater to the defeater. This begins to look like the ordinary state of affairs in the history of epistemology, and the notion of properly basic belief seems only to capture the condition of *prima facie* justification, whereas what has been sought historically is *ultima facie* justification, justification after all things have been considered.

Belief in God arises under certain conditions, just as belief in the external world, according to Plantinga. When appeared to in a certain way, if our noetic equipment is properly functioning, we naturally form the belief that there is a white object before me. So too with belief in God. Seeing the beauty of a sunset, or feeling ashamed of a moral lapse, or receiving a long sought-after prize, one may feel grateful toward God, or humbled before God, or rejoice in the goodness of God to me. But what if I don't? Most of us seem not to dispute that there is a white object before us, but we dispute fiercely that such and such is God's doing. Plantinga has to resort to the notion that a person's noetic equipment may not be functioning properly. Descartes' demon can haunt a dedicated truth seeker, or an Alpha Centauri scientist may conduct experiments on me without my knowing, or a dreaded dendritic disease may afflict me. The reason some do not believe is that their noetic equipment may fail to function properly. Of course, the opposite may be said of the theist by the anti-theist. So, this line of defense does not settle the question of the rationality of religious belief.

Further elaborations of proper function do not help. Plantinga adds to proper functioning faculties, that they must operate in an environment for which they are suited, that the faculties must be designed according to a plan which is aimed at the truth, and the design plan must be a good one, not one designed by one of Hume's lazy angels, but one which has a high probability of achieving its end, namely truth. However, the notion of a design plan begs the question of a designer and cannot be settled in any case. Plantinga's attempt to add an external condition to the internal conditions of justification does not get us closer to the rationality of religious beliefs.

The question of proper function of our faculties becomes an issue only in the case of empirical questions. If it is applied to all of our faculties, especially the faculty of reason, then questions of another sort arise. Is reason reliable in all circumstances or is reason fallible? (By reason is meant the laws of thought.) Is reason ontological and transcendental? (For an answer to these questions, see earlier discussion on reason.) If the laws of thought may be questioned, by what can they be questioned, since questioning is thinking and thinking presupposes the laws of thought. And if the laws of thought are given up, then no thought is possible, and nothing can be thought or said. The same fate awaits those who may question reason as coming under the influence of the fallen condition of man.

How does Plantinga handle the defeater arguments against theism? In the case of the problem of evil, Plantinga shows that evil is not contradictory to the goodness and power of God. There may be a good reason why God allows 13 turps of evil to exist, even if we do not know that reason. In doing so, Plantinga blocks one form of the objection against theism based on evil. But Hume had long before allowed that there may be an easy solution to the problem of evil. The problem of evil is to know why there is evil. Plantinga's strategy is purely defensive. It does not answer why. To show theism is not incoherent, or not any worse off than the beliefs of the antitheist is not to show that theism is rational in any strong sense of the word. It does not show that anti-theism is unwarranted or inexcusable. It does not get to the clarity of general revelation and the inexcusability of unbelief. In leaving matters there, the theist is not yet able to show the reality of moral evil and the necessity of redemptive revelation in which she so ardently believes.

A FILLIP TO APPEASE GETTIER

Any student of philosophy in graduate school is made to wrestle with problems of epistemology. In the last few decades of the twentieth century, they have been made to wrestle with the "Gettier" problem, and with the mind-body problem as it has come to be expressed in the puzzle of "the brain in the vat." What can be said after several decades of exposure to these problems? Why were they problems and do they have to be problems?

The thesis of this work is that some things are clear, and that clarity is possible at the basic level, by attention to uncritically held assumptions. How does this thesis apply to the pains and labors of graduate students in the recent past?

Edmund Gettier (1927–2021) challenged the received definition of knowledge as justified true belief by posing clever counterexamples, which suggested a need for revision of the definition. This is an example of arguing from a particular known to a general definition of knowledge. Others could as well begin with other examples and get to other definitions of knowledge. How are examples to be chosen? Must the definition of knowledge be left to arbitrary selection of starting points?

No one would argue that Gettier's examples are not instances of empirical claims. And no one would argue that these claims are basic claims. Whatever the outcome of Gettier's counterexamples, they do not affect claims which are more basic, claims about whether there is an external world, and about what is real, claims which are the historic concern of philosophy. In that regard, Gettier's problem is not logically or psychologically relevant to what has been important in philosophy. The time and effort expended on Gettier is a case of straining at gnats and swallowing camels.

One could easily adjust to the demands of clever counterexamples by either holding the definition of knowledge and disallow one has knowledge in Gettier's counterexamples. We can say we do not have knowledge in many empirical claims, because of the problem of special cases where unusual circumstances obtain. We do not have strong justification. Or we can grant that this is a case of knowledge as far as empirical claims go, but lower the level of justification needed to weak justification. In which case, the problem and solution depend on a quibble over the meaning of justification, as to whether weak or strong justification is meant in empirical claims.

The brain in the vat problem has more basic issues which need to be answered in order for it to be resolved. Is the mind and the brain one and the same? Is the nature of mind and brain activity logically distinct? Can a neural impulse be identical with a mental image? If the mind is not the brain, that changes the significance of the question.

The second part of the assumption is whether there is an external world which is the cause of what I see, or whether some other mind (God, alien, demon, scientist) is the cause of what I see. This too can be answered if we allow the self-evidence of intentions. What is left over is a rather restricted empirical set of questions, of the Gettier sort, for which a fillip is a sufficient answer.

Chapter 22

———

CRITICAL THEORY

C RITICAL THEORY (1930's–2000's) IS A NEO-MARXIST worldview that is known for its Social Justice movement and related Critical Race Theory. Karl Marx (1818–1883) is a precursor to neo-Marxism. And before Marx were the ancient views of the Hebrews and Greeks; the Judeo-Christian West; The Reformation and Enlightenment; Rationalism and Empiricism; and Kant and Hegel. History unfolds in the context of challenge and response. The Modern and Postmodern periods have left many unresolved disputes that may be met by addressing assumptions and avoiding views that deny that some things are clear.

MARXISM

Instead of building on the common ground principle of clarity affirmed at the high-water mark of the Reformation,[1] the Enlightenment builders sought, through Rationalism (reason alone) and Empiricism (sense experience alone), to lay a new foundation for knowledge and universal cultural authority. Descartes' *cogito* of the self as thinking substance/individual unraveled as Leibniz spun out the implications of substance in the notion of windowless monads, operating in sync by pre-established harmony. His disciple, Christian Wolff (1679–1754), elevated the principle of sufficient reason to deduce the particulars reserved for divine sovereignty in providence. Constructive reason, without the prior critical use of reason, reached its *reductio*.

In England, post-Reformation Enlightenment began with Lockean empiricism, which failed to distinguish primary (objective) qualities

---

1. *Westminster Confession of Faith*, 1.1

from secondary (subjective) qualities (color from size). Bishop Berkeley made all qualities subjective and, therefore, could affirm only mind and its ideas exist. Only God, as primary cause, operates. Hume emptied causality of all objectivity, lost the notion of substance and of the self as knowable by sense experience. The burden of proof fell upon and against theists to show there is an all good and all powerful God.

Enter Kant to the rescue from skepticism, from both rationalism (Wolff) and empiricism (Hume). Necessity in thought comes from forms of outer intuition (time and space) and from categories of the intellect (substance and causality). These belong to the world of appearances (*phenomena*), not the world as it is in itself (*noumena*). By making "cause" mind-dependent, he dismisses all argument from effect (in the world) to cause in God. But cause cannot be dismissed by sophistry. There is a cause of what I see (*phenomena*) in the noumenal realm. There is a chair-in-itself unless one dismisses the idea of self and consciousness, Descartes' starting point. The unknowable *noumena* merely deepens into skepticism.

Hegel posited as the *noumena* an immanent Spirit unfolding in history toward self-consciousness through human consciousness. The individual self is merely a part of the whole; the process is dialectical: conflict (of thesis and antithesis) resolving by a synthesis of the two, which generates its own new antithesis. The goal is freedom. Marx responds in antithesis to Hegel. He accepts the idea of the whole, the idea of the dialectic, and the goal of freedom (liberation). But the process is material (specifically economic) not that of Spirit. Dialectical materialism produces human consciousness (spirit), not the other way around.

Kant's *noumenal* solution to pseudo-skepticism, Hegel's dialectic solution to a pseudo-noumena, and Marx's material solution to a pseudo-dialectic sealed the fate of millions in the 20th century in the name of enlightened human liberation.

Marx defines religion as the opiate of the people. To address this judgment, we must ask: what is religion? Is this true of all, some, none? Does a false view of hope, due to a false view of God, lead to no hope (opium is the religion of the people)? Marx explains religion in terms of economics. He reduces (any supernatural) thought to "material/economic" process in a conflicting dialectic. This is a basic move to reverse the body/soul relation. He does not recognize economic practice in terms of belief. He thinks if work is changed (environment), then one's belief will change. Yet, change in the outward condition will not change the inward condition (beliefs). Marx's view is that all struggle is a power struggle. It is necessary to be non-cognitive and practical first; therefore, Marxism consistently uses force over reason through violent revolution (vs. reformation). Ideas are useful only in service to power, politics, and ideology. Man does not, and cannot, change by truth, understanding meaning, change of mind, or repentance.

There is no personal immortality, and no hope beyond the grave, except for the collective, in Marxism. This builds on Spinoza's view of God as nature, which depends upon an ontological (vs. ethical) unity. For Marx, all is matter (material monism). He does not recognize spirit. He speaks of all religion, but does not recognize the difference between theistic and non-theistic religion, and the admixtures between them. Marx draws the line between matter and spirit rather than recognizing temporal and eternal (all vs. only some is eternal as difference in religion). There is never pure theism and never pure atheism. There is always an admixture of both belief and unbelief with differing levels of consciousness and consistency. Marx's philosophical foundation is empiricism (sense experience), which denies anything is clear to reason. Marx denies that all persons are equally created, all are equally fallen, and equally called through the curse.

Marx has become the ideological poster child of civilizational anti-theism atheism, the current head of the many-headed beast waging war against the City of God through the millennia. Neo-Marxism is the face of that Beast in the current culture war. It is of the Beast to use force (vs. reason) in violent revolution from its rootedness in dialectical materialism, bloodied in the killing of untold millions in its attempt to create the "new man," to inhabit the utopian City of Man. The fundamental falsehood of atheism, rooted in the epistemological absurd, can persuade the masses for a while, but in due time a banner is raised up against it. Some professing theism have been drawn by the voice of the wolf in sheep's clothing in "so called justice," but as the light of what is clear to reason dawns, the shadows fade away. The darkness cannot overcome (or withstand) the light of reason.

SOCIALISM AND VIRTUE ETHICS

Attempts are made to argue for capitalism vs. socialism in the context of virtue ethics—for a free and virtuous society. Empirical evidence is given to show capitalism has increased the material well-being of society significantly more than socialism. Yet socialists do not turn to capitalism. Why? It is suggested they are locked into ideology. But there are other things to consider besides ideology.

Virtue ethics may consider the common good defined in terms of material well-being. The common good is not, however, the good. And material well-being is not an end in itself, but a means to the good. Virtue itself is a means to the good and not the good itself. Apart from the good, virtues may become vices. The pursuit of material well-being apart from the good can become greed, and often does. Some socialists are aware of this.

There are many virtues, and the pursuit of one may be at the expense of others. Liberty in the economic realm may not always be consistent with justice. It may not always be consistent with equality and fraternity, which are other desirable virtues. Socialists value these virtues. The good as the source of unity binds all the virtues together in perfect harmony, for the virtues all aim at the good and are intelligible only in light of the good. So, virtue ethics, by focusing on virtues and not on the good, leaves open the real possibility of conflict among the virtues and, therefore, a standoff between those who uphold differing virtues.

Virtue ethics, by its very nature, has these limits. Without the good, virtue may turn to vice; and without the good, virtues may conflict with each other. The problem was seen in Kant's deontology and the categorical imperative. The solution is not hedonic consequentialism, where happiness (individually or collectively—Hobbes or Mill) is seen as the good. Happiness is the effect or consequence of possessing what we believe is the good and is not intelligible apart from the good. There has been a long standoff between virtue ethics and hedonism. It continues today in debates between capitalism and socialism. Focus on the good is needed to resolve the conflict. But this in itself can be as perplexing without some more basic things in place, things pertaining to epistemology and to metaphysics. Our view of the good—whatever it may be, is a result of our view of what is real, which in turn is a result of our view of how we know.

Those who would promote a free and virtuous society, especially with an appeal to loyalty to transcendent authority, need to give an account of the good sufficient to prevent virtues from becoming vices and to maintain the virtues in perfect unity.

CRITICAL THEORY

Many have argued against various aspects of Critical Theory as it has come to expression in the culture war. Not much has been addressed to the worldviews behind the culture wars or to the philosophical foundation underlying the worldviews. The culture war is asymmetrical. One side argues for a change in thinking, and the other acts for change in the world (activism). One side speaks for truth and facts, the other sees talk of truth as another aspect of aggression for dominance.

The epistemology of Critical Theory (CT) is non-cognitive. Natural conditions determine thoughts and beliefs. Your view is a matter of your economic or cultural background and thus is neither true nor false. Truth is the result of the process of ongoing, never-ending, left-right antithesis as antinomies (because they share common assumptions). The non-cognitivism of CT (vs. proof) opens the way to psychological persuasion (propaganda) where feeling is truth, one knows by "experience" or through the use of force (totalitarianism, one cannot buy or sell, the mark of the Beast). Further, the non-cognitivism of CT results in revolutionary violence and the use of power vs. "truth" seen as "power play." All players seek power to attain their end in a Hobbesian war of each against all. If truth is based upon feeling, what is the cause of my feeling? Is it bio-chemical? Intuition and background? Worldview?

Critical Theory continues the assumption, inherited from Marx, that religion is the opiate of the masses. CT itself is not an *a priori* position; it is not self-evident; it appears to be ideological dogma; its proponents are dogmatic; it is anti-rational and non-cognitive. Is proof relevant? Is all proof a power play (by everyone everywhere)? Does religion arise from a sense of misery? Are all or some religious? What is the definition of religion? What is belief in God? Why is there suffering? These are basic concepts that, if defined, will help settle these disputes.

Critical Theory continues the Marxist assumption that material/ economic forces determine the course of history. There are economic classes that act out of class consciousness for their economic self-interest. There are those who own the means of production and those who do not. The individual is a product of and belongs to the social whole in contrast to the individual having inalienable rights endowed on individuals by their Creator.

Critical Theory analyzes evil, as Rousseau, as coming from without: "man is born free and everywhere he is in chains," in contrast to the theistic worldview of creation, fall, and redemption. Society corrupts man, not the other way around. Kinds of life originate in an evolutionary struggle for survival; in atheism, each kind is not by special creation. Atheism affirms environmental determinism; theism affirms divine determinism. Power, not truth, determines history. Power, not truth, sets us free in atheism. White privilege is an ideological tool in the neo-Marxist quest for cultural hegemonic supremacy.

The concept of intersectionality, a view that the diversity of cultural minority markers in a person may contribute to one's status as oppressed, is a further development of CT. Out of the assumption that all is a power play and the view that the majority oppresses the minority groups, intersectionality is the means by which the power play may be reversed through the reassertion of minority power. We can acknowledge that there are many dimensions of diversity and ask which dimension has priority.

The many dimensions of human nature are ordered. The larger aspect of human nature is that we are finite, temporal, and changeable in being, wisdom, power, holiness, justice, goodness, and truth. The narrower aspect is that all have belief or unbelief, holiness or unholiness, and righteousness or unrighteousness to varying degrees. There is diversity in human personality between prophetic, priestly, and kingly people to varying degrees. We are a body-soul unity, male and female. We have diverse backgrounds (historic situatedness). And, finally, each person is unique. What is common among all human beings is that we are rational animals. Our rationality is the basis of common ground. By establishing common ground, we can go on to address disputes.

The culture war is a war between cultural atheism (CT) and cultural theism. A culture expresses a worldview, which is built upon a foundation that begins with a cornerstone. The present culture war is the latest expression of an ancient war. There is as much diversity on the Left as on the Right. Both are antinomies—polar opposites—and share common assumptions. By going to the foundation of these assumptions, we can avoid the antinomies of the Left and Right (Hegel's dialectic).

WHITE PRIVILEGE:
Dominion vs. Domination

White Privilege (WP) is current jargon in the culture war. It is a *cri de coeur* used by both the accuser and the accused as part of the debris of cultural neo-Marxism. Atheism is a dogma of Marxism. WP is part of the Left neo-Marxist worldview. It has not been argued for seriously, but it is having increasing serious consequences. We are the product of our environment, nature, the creation (vs. the Creator). WP assumes there is only nature, no God who creates and rules nature. WP is another product of atheistic assumptions in the ongoing spiritual war between belief and unbelief.

All of Providence and all of Scripture declare all blessings flow from God by faith/understanding (mere increase of wealth in itself is not the blessing of God). Satan and his host (in the presence of God) in heaven fell. Elect angels were kept by grace. Satan, in his fall, denied God as eternal Creator and himself as finite, temporal, creature. Adam and Eve, in an ideal environment in the Garden of Eden, fell. They did not seek and understand what was clear to reason about God and man and good and evil. They believed the lies of the Devil. Cain and Abel were brought up by the same parents. Cain denied the need for redemption from sin. He failed to understand vicarious atonement—through the death of another, sin is covered. Abel, by grace, brought the lamb (a sign) as the offering for sin. Ishmael departed from the covenant signified by circumcision (the need for regeneration). Isaac, by grace, continued in the covenant, submitting to his father's offering sacrifice, signifying the sacrifice for sin. They both were taught by the same father. Esau and Jacob were twins. Jacob, by grace, had regard for the blessing of God's promise; Esau sold his birthright for a bowl of stew. Joseph differed with his brothers, by grace.

In every age, a remnant is kept by grace. Descendants who depart first abuse, then lose the inherited privileges of grace. In every age, salvation (the blessing of life) is, by grace, sovereignly bestowed, not by works, of ourselves, or by anything in the creation. Good is by God upholding us in the means of grace; Evil is by man acting against his own nature as a finite, temporal, and changeable, rational creature, made in the image of God, with the ability and responsibility to know God.

The charge of White Privilege has several parts. What you have as a white person was handed to you, not earned. It confuses privileges from wealth with ethnicity. Many white people are without economic privileges. Original Marxism drew the line of privilege between the haves and the have-nots; neo-Marxism drew the lines along various minority identities.

Minorities who affirm majority opinions have false consciousness, a pointed problem for neo-Marxist intuitional epistemology. Only minorities know what it feels like to be oppressed. The minority's feelings cannot be described (supposedly), and the majority cannot understand what they do not understand. But appeal to knowledge by an intuitional experience is not meaningful without interpretation. And feeling/experience can and has been interpreted in many ways because of multiple and shifting identities. One's identity can be (and has been) fluid.

Economic increase by dominion (over nature, by cooperation) is not a zero-sum transaction. Economic increase by domination (over others) is a fixed sum. Increasing total wealth by dominion is not re-distribution by domination.

Moral evil originates in unbelief and comes to expression in all unrighteousness and the injustices of domination. Both good and evil grow in a corporate, cumulative, and communal context. As dominion increases over unbelief, domination in every form is made to decrease.

CONCLUSION

There is a culture war between the culture of theism and the culture of atheism. It is a spiritual war between belief and unbelief. We are more or less conscious and consistent in our basic beliefs. The spiritual war is first within each person, according to the measure of one's maturity, in every relation of life. It is the war between good and evil, between basic differences in understanding good and evil.

In Christian theism, God creates humans equally as the image of God. Humans are finite, temporal, and changeable, in being, wisdom, power, holiness, justice, goodness, and truth, with the ability and responsibility to know. Humans differ from animals in our capacity to think (using concepts, judgments, and arguments vs. perceive with the senses) about God the Creator. In Christian theism, all humans are equally fallen: no one seeks; no one understands; all are equally in sin and death in unbelief. All humans are equally called back by the curse and promise: toil and strife, and old age, sickness, and death. The spiritual war is age-long and agonizing until good overcomes evil. All are called to repent of unbelief—the Kingdom of God is at hand. All who repent are equally received by God and the Church, the body of Christ. As members of the body of Christ, each has different gifts and abilities to build up the body of Christ (there are many members, but one body). All members are to be equally discipled. All nations are to be baptized and taught to observe all that Christ has commanded. All members are not equally mature in their faith/understanding. Without the first principles/foundation, a believer does not grow to maturity. What is clear to the believer is foolishness to the unbeliever without faith.

The Gospel calls men everywhere to repent of sin, and the root sin of not seeking and not understanding what is clear about God and man and good and evil, to receive forgiveness and cleansing of God in Christ, the eternal Word of God incarnate, crucified, risen, and ruling, to advance his kingdom, by his law, in all of life. The war, in our day, is between cultural Marxism and cultural Christianity. Participants in this war are more or less woke or awakened. First, or fundamental, principles make it clear where the lines are drawn.

Philosophical foundations are deepest. Philosophical foundation begins with epistemology, then metaphysics, then ethics. In epistemology, the line is drawn between clarity: some things are clear to reason (knowledge is possible), and nothing is clear (to the senses), versus knowledge is not possible (skepticism) and fideism (belief without proof based on understanding). In metaphysics, the line is drawn between "only some (God) is eternal" or "nothing is eternal" or "all is eternal" (matter, spirit, or both). In ethics, the line is drawn between the good (the end in itself) as based on human nature as fundamentally rational, or the good as not based on human nature, or there is no human nature as such or human nature is not fundamentally rational. The former leads to the earth filled with the knowledge of God; the latter leads to hedonism (pleasure is the good), or virtue is the good (deontology) and is rewarded by some form or other of non-cognitive mysticism.

Both sides in the culture war are divided depending on how conscious, and consistent each is. Without a clear view of good and evil, divisions deepen. The greater the clarity, the greater the unity.

Marx is a child of Enlightenment skepticism and the poster child of postmodern skepticism. From the divisions of Descartes and Locke to Wolff and Hume, Kant's response deepened skepticism by dividing *phenomena* and *noumena*. His analysis of causality as only subjectively real was disingenuous. He failed to recognize the causal relation between *noumena* as the cause of *phenomena*. In morality, his libertarian free will (*ought* implies *can* vs. *want*) required the denial of causality to make room for freedom for morality—a double error.

Hegel supplied a view of Spirit (pantheistic *noumena*) unfolding history (*phenomena*) by a supposedly rational process of dialectic between ideas—thesis, antithesis, synthesis. He assumed, without argument, Kant's skepticism, his unknowable God, and the redefinition of religion as morality (deontology).

Marx assumed and one-upped Hegel by rejecting Spirit by antithesis for a dialectic that was material and in an economic sense, created a dialectic between two classes, the owners (*bourgeoisie*) and workers (*proletariat*). Capitalism (man individually owns absolutely) will be replaced by communism—a classless society in which man collectively owns absolutely.

The struggle is one of power, not truth, for a good that is material, not spiritual, in which those who have do not increase, but take by oppression from those who do not have. There is only distribution, not increase of wealth (Adam Smith), only fairness, not efficiency. Man is born free and noble but is now everywhere in chains (Rousseau). Evil comes from without (we are victims), from an evil class, not from within, by denying one's rational nature (through neglecting, avoiding, resisting, and denying reason). Man is thrown back into a Hobbesian world of incessant class conflict (not of conflict from ethical egoism).

The theory of dialectical materialism based on a purely naturalist (vs. theistic) view of man, having failed to "materialize" after the loss of millions of lives in Russia, China, and South-East Asia, and resisted stoutly in the post-WWII Cold War (1950s–1990s) morphed under German, French, and Italian Marxism into neo-Marxist Critical Theory. Oppression is not only economic, but is based on race and gender, and wherever there is a power disparity by virtue of varying class identities.

Critical Theory denies there is any meta-narrative that is to be privileged (skepticism). Difference is not of truth, which is unknowable because nothing is clear, and there is no essence of human nature to be known. All is a material flux (from the Greek materialists) available only to varying perspectives of the senses (Empiricus, Democritus, Heraclitus, Epicurus), leaving us in skepticism (Protagoras—man is the measure of all things). Claims to truth and objectivity are to be deconstructed and shown to be an ideology used to gain and keep power. It is all a matter of interpretation (construction) as will to power.

The power/oppression narrative can split along any mark of diversity without being able to privilege any (intersectionality). White privilege (in a majority white society) would not be any different from black privilege (in a majority black society) or patriarchy over matriarchy, or straight vs. gay. It is a hopeless power struggle ever-increasing by intersectionality (gay, white, female, poor, educated, non-intellectual) based on skepticism (nothing is clear) and fideistic anti-theism (all is natural/matter). There is no meaning, no possibility of meaning, but driven only by desire in restless boredom to ever-increasing excess and perversion, concerning which no judgment should be made (politically incorrect) without a torrent of abuse of all kinds (the exercise of power without truth).

In the culture war, power seeks to destroy the other and fails only if it self-destructs first. The other side of the culture war (theism), if it can repent of its unbelief that divides, can call the world to repent, for the Kingdom of Heaven is at hand.

GLOSSARY OF TERMS

ambiguity
a term is ambiguous if it has more than one meaning: equivocal—if it has two unrelated meanings (ring on a finger, ring of a bell); analogous—if it has two related meanings (blanket of snow or bed cover); all non-basic terms are also philosophically ambiguous, relative to basic belief; a term is univocal if it has only one meaning.

analogous
like in some respects and unlike in other respects.

antinomy
contrary positions both of which can be false at the same time because both share a common assumption—capitalism and communism; this-worldly and other-worldly; all is eternal and none is eternal; skepticism and fideism; virtue is the good and happiness is the good—a source of recurrent conflict within and between cultures.

argument
the third act of reason (see concept and judgment) in which premises are used to logically support a conclusion (see validity and soundness).

basic belief
a belief is basic in relation to another if it is assumed by that belief; material monism (all is matter) assumes that all is eternal; macro-evolution assumes all is matter; superior race assumes macro-evolution; naturalistic science assumes methodological naturalism, which assumes metaphysical naturalism (all is matter).

clarity
applied to basic beliefs; a belief is clear to reason if the contradiction is not logically or existentially possible; e.g., there must be something eternal; clarity is necessary for meaning, morality, and inexcusability; one knows what is clear if one can show what is clear; what is clear can be known by anyone who seeks to know.

common ground   the set of epistemologically necessary conditions for thought and discourse: 1) reason—as the laws of thought; 2) integrity—as a concern for consistency; 3) Rational Presuppositionalism—as critical thinking applied consistently; 4) the Principle of Clarity—as necessary for meaning and morality; to engage in discourse without common ground is to engage in meaningless disputes.

common sense   takes appearance for reality: the sun rises in the east; the earth is flat; the color of the ocean is blue; there is an external world; based on what is common to sense perception, rather than common sense as practical wisdom; it takes the condition/position of the perceiver for granted.

concept   the first act of reason (see judgment and argument); in a concept the mind grasps the essence of a thing or class of things; set in contrast to an image, an act of the senses; concepts are either well-formed or not.

contradiction   contradictory statements differ in quantity (all or some) and quality (is or is not); they cannot both be true and they cannot both be false, at the same time and in the same respect; *all s is p* is contradicted by *some s is not p*; *no s is p* is contradicted by *some s is p* (see judgment).

creation *ex nihilo*   affirmed by historic theism, it is the belief that God created the world out of no pre-existing substance; in contrast to dualism where creation is by forming pre-existing matter, and to pantheism—in which the world is a part of God; it is the basis of affirming the infinite power and wisdom of God.

deconstruction   recognizes the constructive use of reason by providing an internal conceptual critique of a position; does not apply critical analysis to test the meaning of basic beliefs upon which construction occurs; calls into question reason in itself based upon the mere subjective use of reason.

deduction reasoning from what is more general or universal to what is less general or particular; from all men are mortal to Socrates is mortal; from saying it is true of all to saying it is true of each.

deism belief that the world was created by God, but not actively ruled by God; God did not act after creation to bring about natural evil in the world, or to give any redemptive revelation to mankind (Voltaire and Thomas Jefferson).

deontology a theory of ethics focused upon duty and virtue as the end of moral action, independent of and in contrast to consequences; affirmed by Kant; set in contrast to teleological ethics which sees virtue as means to the good.

determinism the belief that every event has a cause and that given the cause the effect necessarily follows; in contrast to libertarianism; hard determinists affirm causality and deny libertarian freedom; soft determinists affirm causality and freedom as doing what one desires.

dilemma in logic, a form of argumentation in which either of two alternatives available is unacceptable; used rhetorically to show how entirely unacceptable a position is.

dominion the exercise of rule or authority given to mankind to develop the powers latent in oneself and in the creation; based on the principle that creation is revelation, it is directed toward the good as knowledge of God; set in contrast to domination as rule for self-interest.

dualism the ontological position that reality consists of two distinct kinds of being—matter and spirit—both of which are eternal; affirmed in different forms of Greek thought by Plato and Aristotle; distinct from theism, although dualistic attitudes persist in popular forms of theism.

empiricism the epistemological position that all knowledge arises from sense experience; affirmed by John Locke; Hume drew out its skeptical implications; assumed uncritically in some claims made in the name of science; radical empiricism includes inner as well as sense experience.

epistemology   theory of knowledge; a major branch of philosophy that deals with the questions "Is knowledge possible?" and "How do I know?"

essence   the set of qualities that all members and only members of a class always have; human essence is said to be both rational and animal.

ethics   ethics is concerned with giving a rational justification for an answer to the question "What is the good?" Ethics assumes choice, which assumes values and therefore the highest value, which is the good; what is sought in ethics is rational justification for one's view of the good.

evolution, naturalistic   a purely natural explanation of the development from non-life to life, to more complex life, to hominid, to human; macro (not micro) evolution; internal disputes exist over gradual vs. non-gradual process; external challenges exist over the scientific vs. philosophical status of evolution.

evolution, theistic   a synthesis of naturalistic evolution and belief in God; subject to criticism from both naturalists and theists as compromising essential features of each, and is therefore inadequate as a compromise position; it has been subject to revision in the direction of theism or naturalism.

ex nihilo   from no previously existing matter.

existentialism   focus upon the individual in an actual condition of crisis with respect to the absence of any rational way to choose; without God (Nietzsche, Sartre) or without reason (Kierkegaard), man is forced to authentic freedom; his existence precedes what he becomes by choice (essence).

faith   faith is applied to belief in general, which cannot be verified through sense experience; faith is not opposed to reason; as truth cannot be separated from meaning, faith cannot be separated from reason; faith grows as understanding grows; it is tested as understanding is tested.

fideism holding a belief without proof; proof is seen either as not relevant or not possible or may not actually be present; belief may be either theistic or non-theistic; fideism assumes basic things are not clear; belief without proof based on understanding loses all meaning.

freedom doing what I want or please or choose, all things considered; applied to the most basic level of thought, I can use my reason if I want to; set in contrast to libertarian freedom: if *ought* implies *can*, then *can* assumes *want*; the want of a rational agent is always free.

friendship friendship is reciprocal, lasting and shares the deepest concerns; it is therefore the effect of mutual commitment to the good; in contrast to other relations which are not reciprocal, lasting, or cannot share the deepest concerns because they are not based on mutual commitment to the good.

general revelation what can be known of God by all persons, everywhere, at all times, through the ordinary means of knowing; in contrast to special revelation; the subject matter of natural vs. revealed religion.

good and necessary consequence an inference of reason; what must be said, if other things are accepted as true; applied to analyzing concepts, judgments, and arguments; used in critical, interpretive, and constructive reasoning.

happiness the effect of possessing what one believes to be the good; not sought for its own sake as the good, but naturally accompanying the possessing what is believed to be of highest value; lasting happiness is the effect of possessing what truly is the good.

hedonism the ethical view that pleasure/happiness of one kind or another is the good (Epicurus, Mill).

hermeneutics the process by which the meaning of a text or an event is understood; no experience is meaningful without interpretation; in general, we interpret what is less basic in light of what is more basic; we interpret our experience in light of our basic belief or worldview assumptions.

induction   reasoning from observation of instances of things to a general statement about that class of things; from observing that some crows are black to the general statement that all crows are black.

informal fallacy   an attempt to persuade by pseudo-argument (through appeal to what is not rationally relevant) rather than to prove by sound argument: appeal to fear and pity apart from the good; appeal to authority or popularity rather than reason; speaking against the person vs. what was said, etc.

integrity   integrity is grounded in a concern to be whole or unified in one's being; specifically, it is a concern for consistency over and against inconsistency, which is manifest in contradiction in thought; double-mindedness in desire and hypocrisy in what we profess and what we do.

intuition   an immediate awareness one has, apart from reason and the senses, of the connection between a (natural) sign and what it signifies; e.g., smile and friendliness, beauty and goodness; misleading if one thinks the sign is the reality, or that the sign is always accompanied by the reality.

judgment   the second act of reason in which two concepts are joined by affirmation or separated by negation: *all s is p, no s is p, some s is p, some s is not p*; judgments are either true or false and may be simple or complex; a statement is used to express a judgment (or proposition).

knowledge   justified true belief.

libertarianism   a view of freedom where *ought* implies *can*; one is free if one could have done otherwise; related to causality, if my act was caused, it could not have been otherwise; libertarianism denies determinism (every event is caused) in order to affirm freedom (Kant, William James).

literalism   the belief that understanding a text is free of interpretive assumptions; that preceding layers of context are not necessarily relevant; that meaning is explicit only and not also by inference; that understanding language figuratively is to be avoided whenever possible.

love   love seeks the good for the other; love is a moral virtue, not the good sought for its own sake; set in contrast to romantic love in which the other is considered the good; in theism, to seek the good as the knowledge of God is to love God and to love oneself.

matter   that which has size and is not conscious; can be measured.

metaphysics   a branch of philosophy which deals with the question, "What is real or eternal?"; it deals with *ontology*—the nature of being, whether being is matter or spirit; it deals with *cosmology*—how the cosmos came to be.

moral evil   an act contrary to the nature of one's being; for man as a rational being it is to neglect, avoid, resist, or deny reason in the face of what is clear; it is the failure to seek and to understand and to do what is right.

natural evil   in the context of an all powerful and all good Creator, natural evil is not original in the creation, nor inherent in moral evil; it is imposed by God to restrain, recall from, and to remove moral evil; it consists in toil and strife, and old age, sickness, and death, and all amplifications of these in famine, war, and plague.

naturalism   the worldview of material monism: only natural forces explain all phenomena of nature; applied to human culture, it is called secular humanism: only human effort explains all social phenomena; in the sciences, methodological naturalism in explanation (all knowledge is through sense experience) is used to support metaphysical naturalism—there is no God, no spirit or soul, and no afterlife.

nihilism   the loss of all meaningful distinctions in epistemology, metaphysics, and ethics; the inherent consequence of skepticism—the denial of all clarity; a position which cannot be maintained with integrity.

ontology   the study of being.

philosophy   philosophy can be defined in terms of its several features: *area*—foundation and goal; *attitude*—love of wisdom; *method*—critical use of reason; *application*—self-examination; *system*—a worldview.

postmodern   a cluster of skeptical responses to claims to objective truth in modern thought; it is anti-foundationalism, anti-realism, and anti-essentialism; it assumes reason is not ontological or transcendental, nor is thinking presuppositional; it privileges the subjective aspects of interpretation.

pragmatism   a theory of truth: a belief is true if it yields satisfactory consequences (if it works); also, a theory of meaning: the meaning of a belief is the conduct it is fitted to produce (William James); claims to settle metaphysical disputes; assumes skepticism and that what works is common ground.

presupposi-   what is assumed or presupposed in any given statement
tion   or belief; applied particularly to what is assumed in a person's *system* of beliefs or worldview; one's most basic belief about what is eternal.

prima facie   literally "on the face of it"; applied to epistemic justification, rights, duties, evidence, etc.; it leaves open the question of who bears the burden of proof and what is one's epistemic duty: is one obligated to search out objections before believing what is *prima facie* justified?

problem   if God is all good and all powerful, why is there evil?; if
of evil   God is all powerful, he could create a world without evil; if he is all good, he would create a world without evil; the problem is intellectual, to make sense of an apparent contradiction, and not empty basic terms of meaning.

rational presupposi- tionalism	thinking is presuppositional; we think of the less basic in light of the more basic: less basic/more basic, truth/ meaning, experience/basic belief, conclusion/premises, finite/infinite, etc.; reason is the test for meaning; if we agree on what is more basic, we can agree on what is less basic.
rationalism	a reliance on reason as the source of knowing the truth; to be contrasted with reliance on sense experience or intuition or testimony; also, to be contrasted with reli- ance on reason as a test for meaning (rational presup- positionalism).
reason in its use	reason in its use is *formative*—used to form concepts, judgments, and arguments, which are the forms of all thought; *critical*—used as a test of meaning; *inter- pretive*—used to interpret experience in light of basic belief; and *constructive*—used to construct a coher- ent worldview.
reason in itself	reason in itself is the laws of thought: the law of iden- tity—*a is a*; the law of non-contradiction—*not both a and non-a*; the law of excluded middle—*either a or non-a*; these laws make thinking possible; the common ground for all who think.
reason in us	reason in us is *natural*—the same in all thinkers; *ontolog- ical*—applies to being as well as to thought; *transcenden- tal*—authoritative, self-attesting, cannot be questioned but makes questioning possible; and *fundamental*—to all other aspects of human personality.
redemptive revelation	scripture as redemptive revelation reveals how man is brought out of sin and death; scripture assumes all have sinned—no one seeks, no one understands, no one is righteous; all are in the state of spiritual death—mean- inglessness, boredom, and guilt; redemption by vicar- ious atonement shows both divine justice and mercy.

reductio ad absurdum	a form of reasoning which proves the truth of a position by showing the opposite cannot be true because it is reduced to logical absurdity; used to show there must be something eternal; used to show the strong sense of clarity necessary to establish inexcusability.
religion	the belief or set of beliefs used to give meaning to experience.
science	the attempt to increase knowledge of reality based on theory confirmed by observation in experiment; science is overextended and becomes a source of skepticism when it assumes empiricism, that all knowledge is from sense experience, or makes claims which go beyond experience.
sensus divinitatis	the immediate awareness of divinity present in human consciousness; variously understood, ranging from a sense of dependence on a higher power to awareness of God as Creator and ruler, or as one having an innate sense of the qualities of infinite, eternal, and unchanging, which can only, upon analysis, be applied to God.
skepticism	the epistemological view that knowledge is not possible, that nothing is clear; consistently held, skepticism leads to nihilism, the loss of all meaning.
Sola Scriptura	a principle of authority which maintains that scripture is the only rule of faith and life; set in contrast to new revelations of the Spirit or traditions of men; not set in contrast to reason making inferences from scripture, nor to reason making judgments concerning circumstances common to human societies.
soundness	an argument is sound if it is valid and its premises are true (see argument and validity); a rational person will believe the conclusion of a sound argument.
special revelation	what is known of God through testimony and its transmission; usually contained in form of scripture; the subject matter of revealed theology in contrast to natural theology or religion.

spirit that which has no size and is conscious (also known as mind, soul, or consciousness).

spiritual monism the ontological position that all of reality is eternal and is spirit; set in contrast to material monism, dualism, and theism; matter only *appears* to exist; this reality may be absolute non-dual, beyond all qualities (Shankara) or qualified non-dual, where all is part of God (Ramanuja).

spiritual death set in contrast to and analogous to physical death; the inward condition of meaninglessness, boredom, and guilt; inherent in moral evil as the failure to seek and to understand basic things that are clear to reason.

talent an ability to achieve some aspect of the good; originating in one's being and unique in each; developed fully only in the vision of the good; it is given to each for all; the good, achieved by talent, is the source of lasting value and of the richness of life for all.

term a word or group of words used to express a concept (see concept, essence, and ambiguity).

the good the good is the end in itself, chosen for its own sake and not for the sake of anything else; it is the highest good (*the summum bonum*); it is the source of unity (in a person, between two persons, and between groups of persons); set in contrast to virtue as means to the good and happiness as the effect of possessing the good.

the principle of clarity some things are clear, the basic things are clear, the basic things about God and man and good and evil are clear to reason; necessary for meaning and morality.

theism belief in God the Creator who brought the universe and all things in it into being; God is a Spirit, infinite, eternal, and unchangeable, in his being, wisdom, power, holiness, justice, goodness, and truth; in contrast to deism, God in theism is both Creator and ruler of mankind in history.

tradition	a way of life handed down by and received on the basis of testimony, in contrast to reason, intuition, or sense experience; without critical analysis, traditions are affirmed to be equal, requiring radical pluralism, diversity, multiculturalism, cultural relativism, and tolerance.
transcendental	that which is higher; stands above; authoritative.
uniformitarianism	a principle which holds that the forces now operating in nature have always operated, and in essentially the same magnitude; a naturalistic assumption first used in geology by Charles Lyell, and in biology by Charles Darwin.
utilitarianism	holds that pleasure is the good and that we are to act so as to maximize the greatest amount of pleasure for the greatest number of people; proposed by Jeremy Bentham and John Stuart Mill; set in contrast to ethical egoism—one should seek pleasure for oneself first, and to deontology—duty for duty's sake.
validity	an argument is valid if its premises logically support the conclusion (see argument and soundness).
virtue	virtue is not the good, but the means to the good; there are different kinds of virtues: instrumental (money, house, car), natural (health, beauty, talent), and moral (wisdom, courage, love).
wisdom	knowing the good and the appropriate means to achieving the good.
worldview	how a person understands the world based on answers to the basic questions; each culture is shaped by a worldview held more or less consciously and consistently; a culture grows or declines as its worldview increases or decreases in its capacity to provide meaning.

BIBLIOGRAPHY

Aquinas, Thomas. *Summa Theologica*. Edited by Mortimer J. Adler. Vol. 19 of *Great Books of the Western World,* edited by Mortimer J. Adler. Chicago: Encyclopedia Britannica, 1955.

Aristotle. *Complete Works of Aristotle: The Revised Oxford Translation*. Edited by J. Barnes. 2 vols. Bollingen Series. Princeton, NJ: Princeton University Press, 1983.

———. *The Nicomachean Ethics*. Edited by Hugh Tredennick. Translated by J.A.K. Thomas. New York: Penguin Group, 2004.

———. *Philosophy of Aristotle*. Translated by Renford Bambrough, J.L. Creed and A.E. Wardman. New York: Penguin Group, 2003.

Augustine. *Concerning the City of God Against the Pagans*. Translated by Henry Bettenson. London: Penguin Books, 1984.

———. *Confessions*. Translated by Henry Chadwick. Oxford: Oxford University Press, 1991.

Bennett, Jonathan. *Learning From Six Philosophers: Descartes, Spinoza, Leibniz, Locke, Berkeley, Hume*. Oxford: Oxford University Press, 2003.

Berkeley, George B. *Berkeley's Three Dialogues between Hylas and Philonous*. Edited by Colin M. Turbayne. New York: The Liberal Arts Press, 1954.

Burton, Kelly Fitzsimmons. *Retrieving Knowledge: A Socratic Response to Skepticism*. Phoenix: Public Philosophy Press, 2018.

Calvin, John. *The Institutes of the Christian Religion*. Translated and edited by Ford Lewis Battles. Grand Rapids, MI: W.B. Eerdmans, 1987.

Camus, Albert. *The Myth of Sisyphus and Other Essays*. Translated by Justin O'Brien. New York: Knopf Publishing Group, 1991.

Cornford, Frances Macdonald. *Before and After Socrates*. Cambridge: Cambridge University Press, 1932.

Cornford, Francis Macdonald. *Plato's Theory of Knowledge: The Theaetetus and the Sophist of Plato*. London: Routledge, 2000.

Derrida, Jacques and Gayatri Chakravorty Spivak. *Of Grammatology*. Baltimore: Johns Hopkins University Press, 1998.

Descartes, René, Elizabeth Sanderson Haldane, and G.R.T. Ross. *A Discourse on Method and Meditations.* Mineola, NY. Dover Publications, Incorporated, 2003.

Deutsch, Eliot. *Advaita Vedanta: A Philosophical Reconstruction.* Honolulu: University of Hawaii Press, 1969.

———, trans. *The Bhagavad Gita.* New York: Holt, Rinehart and Winston, 1968.

Empiricus, Sextus. *Selections from the Major Writings on Scepticism, Man, and God.* Edited by Phillip P. Hallie. Translated by Sanford G. Etheridge. Middletown, CT: Wesleyan University Press, 1964.

Gangadean, Ashok K. *Meditative Reason—Toward Universal Grammar.* New York: Peter Lang, 1993.

———. *Between Worlds: The Emergence of Global Reason.* New York: Peter Lang, 1998.

Gangadean, Surrendra. *Philosophical Foundation: A Critical Analysis of Basic Beliefs, Second Edition.* Phoenix: Public Philosophy Press, 2022.

———. *The Logos Papers: To Make the Logos Known.* Phoenix: Logos Papers Press, 2022.

Gettier, Edmund L. "Is Justified True Belief Knowledge?" *Analysis* 23, no. 6 (1963): 121.

Grant, Colin. "Anselm's Argument Today." *Journal of the American Academy of Religion* 57, no. 4 (Winter, 1989): 791-806.

Hart, Hendrik, Johan Van Der Hoeven, and Nicholas Wolterstorff, eds. *Rationality in the Calvinian Tradition.* Lanham, MD: University Press of America, 1983.

Herman, Arthur. *The Cave and the Light: Plato Versus Aristotle, and the Struggle for the Soul of Western Civilization.* New York: Random House, 2014.

Hegel, Georg Wilhelm Friedrich. *Lectures on the Philosophy of World History.* Translated by H.B. Nisbet. Cambridge: Cambridge University Press, 1975.

Heidegger, Martin, and Richard Taft. *Kant and the Problem of Metaphysics.* Bloomington, IN: Indiana University Press, 1997.

Hume, David. *Dialogues and Natural History of Religion.* Edited by J.C.A. Gaskin. Oxford: Oxford University Press, 1993.

———. *Enquiries Concerning Human Understanding.* 3rd ed. New York: Oxford University Press, 1975.

———. *A Treatise on Human Nature.* Edited with an analytical index by L.A. Selby Bigge Oxford, Clarendon Press, 1888.

Inwood, Michael J. *Hegel Selections.* New York: Prentice Hall, 1997.

Kant, Immanuel. *Critique of Pure Reason.* Edited by Howard Caygil. Translated by Norman Kemp Smith. New York: St. Martin's Press, 1965.

———. *Fundamental Principles of the Metaphysic of Morals.* New York: Bobbs-Merrill Company, Inc., 1949.

Kierkegaard, Soren. *Fear and Trembling* and *The Sickness Unto Death.* Translated by Walter Lowrie. Princeton: Princeton University Press, 1954.

———. *Concluding Unscientific Postscript.* Translated and edited by Howard V. Hong and Edna H. Hong. Princeton: Princeton University Press, 1992.

Laertius, Diogenes., trans. Pamela Mensch., ed. Lives of the Eminent Philosophers. New York: Oxford University Press, 2018.

Leibniz, G.W., *Discourse on Metaphysics and the Monadology.* Edited by George R. Montgomery, and Albert R. Chandler. Mineola, NY: Dover Publications, 2005.

Locke, John. *An Essay Concerning Human Understanding.* Edited by Peter H. Nidditch. Oxford: Clarendon Press, 1975.

Markus, R. A., ed. *Augustine: A Collection of Critical Essays.* New York: Doubleday Anchor, 1972.

Marx, Karl. *Capital.* Translated by David McLellan. Oxford: Oxford University Press, 1999.

———. *The Communist Manifesto.* Edited by Friedrich Engels. Translated by David McLellan. Oxford: Oxford University Press, 1998.

McLellan, David. *Marxism After Marx.* Hants, Wales: Macmillan Publishers Limited, 1998.

Mill, John Stuart. *Utilitarianism.* Mineola, NY: Dover Publications, 2007.

Nietzsche, Friedrich. *The Portable Nietzsche.* Translated by Walter Kaufmann. New York: Penguin Group, 1977.

O'Connor, D.J., ed. *A Critical History of Western Philosophy.* New York: Free Press, 1985.

Plantinga, Alvin. *Warrant: The Current Debate.* Oxford: Oxford University Press, 1993.

———. *Warrant and Proper Function.* Oxford: Oxford University Press, 1993.

———. *Warranted Christian Belief.* Oxford: Oxford University Press, 2000.

Plato. *Complete Works: Plato.* Edited by John M. Cooper and D.S. Hutchinson. Indianapolis, IN: Hackett Publishing Company, 1997.

————. *The Republic.* Translated by Francis Macdonald Cornford. Oxford: Oxford University Press, 1951.

Radhakrishnan, Sarvepalli and Charles A. Moore. *Sourcebook in Indian Philosophy.* Princeton: Princeton University Press, 1967.

Ross, David and John Lloyd Ackrill. *Aristotle.* London: Routledge, 2004.

Sartre, Jean-Paul. *Existentialism and Human Emotions.* New York: Kensington Publishing Corporation, 2000.

Shankara. *The Vedanta Sutras of Badarayana with the Commentary by Shankara, Volumes 1and 2.* Translated by George Thibaut. New York: Dover Publication, 1962.

Sharma, Chandradhar. *A Critical Survey of Indian Philosophy.* Delhi, India: Motilal Banarsidass Publishers, 1991.

Spinoza, Benedictus de. *The Collected Works of Spinoza.* Translated and edited by Edwin Curley. Princeton, NJ: Princeton University Press, 1985.

Suzuki, D.T. and C.G. Jung. *An Introduction to Zen Buddhism.* New York: Grove/Atlantic, 1987.

Wheelwright, Phillip, ed. *The Presocratics.* New York: Odyssey Press, 1966.

Young, William. *Hegel's Dialectical Method.* Nutley, NJ: Craig Press, 1972.

Zeller, Eduard. *Outlines of the History of Greek Philosophy.* Mineola, NY: Dover Publications, 1980.

INDEX

ABOUT THE AUTHOR

DR. SURRENDRA GANGADEAN was professor of Philosophy at Phoenix College and at Paradise Valley Community College for forty-five years. He regularly taught courses in Introduction to Philosophy, Logic, Ethics, Philosophy of Religion, History of World Religions, and Introduction to Christianity. For ten years, he taught courses in the History of Eastern Civilizations and in Interdisciplinary Humanities. In addition, he taught courses in Philosophy of Art, Philosophy of Literature, Philosophy of History, and Theology. He led seminar discussions for faculty, students, and the public in the Great Books Reading and Discussion Program. He received an M.A. degree in Literature from Arizona State University, an M.A. degree in Philosophy from the University of Arizona, and a Ph.D. in Natural Theology from Reformed International Theological Seminary. He presented academic papers and public lectures on the topics of Natural Theology and the Moral Law.